PUBLISHED IN AUSTRALIA IN 2016 BY
THE IMAGES PUBLISHING GROUP PTY LTD
ABN 89 059 734 431
6 BASTOW PLACE, MULGRAVE, VICTORIA 3170, AUSTRALIA
TEL: +61 3 9561 5544 FAX: +61 3 9561 4860
BOOKS@IMAGESPUBLISHING.COM
WWW.IMAGESPUBLISHING.COM

COPYRIGHT © THE IMAGES PUBLISHING GROUP PTY LTD 2016
THE IMAGES PUBLISHING GROUP REFERENCE NUMBER: 1142

IN ASSOCIATION WITH
PATRICK TIGHE ARCHITECTURE
5747 VENICE BLVD
LOS ANGELES, CA 90019, UNITED STATES
+1 323 424 7594
WWW.TIGHEARCHITECTURE.COM

BOOK DESIGN BY STUDIO ROXANE ZARGHAM

NATIONAL LIBRARY OF AUSTRALIA CATALOGUING-IN-PUBLICATION ENTRY:

TITLE: PATRICK TIGHE ARCHITECTURE: BUILDING DICHOTOMY / PATRICK TIGHE (AUTHOR).
ISBN: 9781864706758 (HARDBACK)
NOTES: INCLUDES BIBLIOGRAPHICAL REFERENCES.
SUBJECTS: PATRICK TIGHE ARCHITECTURE (FIRM)
              ARCHITECTURE—UNITED STATES.
              ARCHITECTURAL DESIGN—UNITED STATES.

DEWEY NUMBER: 720.973

PATRICK
TIGHE
ARCHITECTURE

BUILDING DICHOTOMY

ESSAYS
BY THOM MAYNE
AND STEPHEN PHILLIPS

BUILDING DICHOTOMY

The buildings were gray. The sky was gray. A gray aura hung over the place. Lowell, Massachusetts, where I was born and raised a first-generation American, was a depressed mill town. My father was a bricklayer, who built in concrete and stone and worked on buildings similar to those that defined the character of the city.

This is where I first encountered the work of the architectural firm Morphosis through their first monograph. I was astounded to see that architecture was not merely a technical discipline, but had an equally important creative component. Most surprising to me were the ways in which the information was communicated. I was transfixed by the new modes of representation and in particular, by the innovative use of drawing. In an instant, the practice of architecture seemed within reach.

At twenty-two, I packed my car and drove as far west as possible. Los Angeles, with all its allure, offered a different perspective and an abundance of new experiences. The city of Angels proved to be an intriguing counterpoint to Lowell. For me, it was similar to a David Hockney painting: Contemporary, with modern, clean lines, vivid colors, palm trees, and a pool disturbed only by a splash from an unknown source. Subscribing to the outsider's fantasy, I was seduced by the difference. The dichotomy of these two places begins to tell the story of our Architecture: our work draws from and builds upon polarities.

PATRICK TIGHE

Today, Los Angeles is no longer a stranger. It is the home base of our practice, a testing ground, and a constant source of inspiration. Our Los Angeles location allows us to benefit from the abundant collaborative spirit among the varied creative disciplines with their diverse points of view. In addition, a palpable energy exists here that is inevitably reflected in our buildings and projects. The past decade has marked the advent and advancement of our practice and coincides with the transformation of a burgeoning city coming into its own. Los Angeles is the platform from which our work is transported. Our ideas have expanded beyond just the city and are now being realized globally.

The one constant in our work is our approach—a pushing of extremes. We identify dichotomies and draw from them—expanding some, mitigating others. Through this process, the essence of each project is distilled and ultimately made clear. Armed with this knowledge we create our Architecture.

We identify and draw from dichotomies to find resolution in our work.

We embrace rather than resolve, conflict. Tension yields a more dynamic architecture.

We value the role that other disciplines and points of view play in our architecture.

We thrive on the cultural exchange of ideas.

We advocate new means of fabrication, materials research, and the digital.

We always integrate new modes of representation in our work.

We place great value on the idea behind each project and ensure that it is made manifest in what is, ultimately, the most important part of our practice, the built work.

In every instance, we embrace dichotomy, mining its potential to produce a more vital and consequential architecture.

The work is situated in the following five areas, each allowing us to move forward with design in a unique and compelling way.

CRAFT
From the manufactured to the technological.

MATERIAL
From the natural to the synthetic.

EXPERIENCE
From the actual to the perceptual.

GEOMETRY
From the simple to the complex.

METHOD
From the analog to the digital.

MANUFACTURED

BLACK BOX
Santa Monica, California

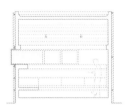

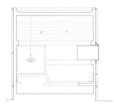

OUT OF MEMORY
Los Angeles, California

CRAFT
FROM THE MANUFACTURED
TO THE TECHNOLOGICAL

We design, draw, compute, and make.

Our interest in making ranges from technologically advanced fabrication techniques to those that are handcrafted. Decisions regarding "how we make" in each project drive the way that the work is realized. Fabricating and prototyping play critical roles in its evolution.

Out of Memory, an installation for the SCI-Arc gallery in Los Angeles, was an investigation into robotic fabrication exploring the potential of robotic milling where the robot was used as an integral part of the construction process. We examined the use of integrated tooling techniques and employed custom software to realize the three-dimensional representation of sound within the immersive installation space.

At the other end of the spectrum, the Black Box is a modest structure built by tradespeople using the simplest construction methods.

NATURAL

TRAHAN RANCH
Austin, Texas

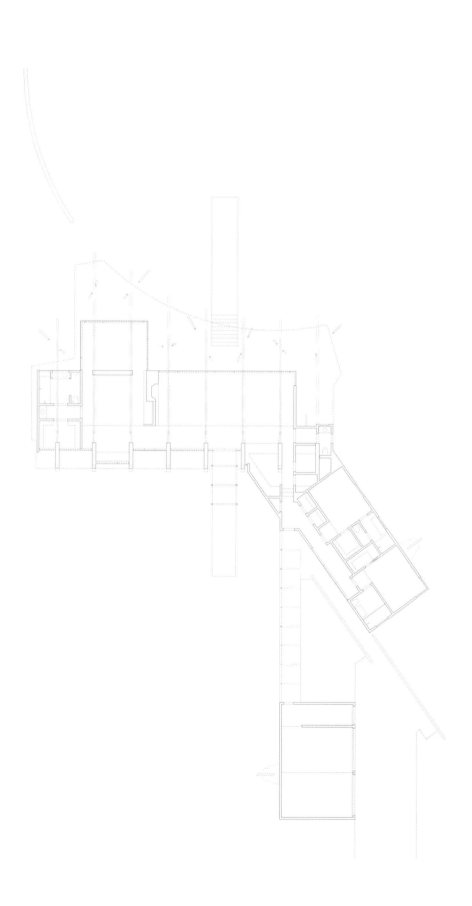

MATERIAL
FROM THE NATURAL
TO THE SYNTHETIC

Material choices are always in sync with design intentions.

The chosen material and its application inform, drive, and ultimately become the architecture. Often, unremarkable materials used in unexpected ways contribute to the success of a project. Equally important is the research and development of innovative new materials, each having its own integrity.

For Trahan Ranch in Austin, Texas, we employed locally sourced materials. A palette of steel, wood, stone, concrete, and glass comprise the hillside home. Limestone mined from the site and cedar felled from the Texas Hill Country feature prominently.

In contrast, the Spray On House explores the potential of renewable polyurethane spray-on foam. Recent advancements in foam technology and the need for more sustainable building solutions render this material well suited for innovative construction applications.

SYNTHETIC

SPRAY ON HOUSE
Joshua Tree, California

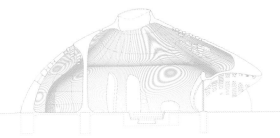

ACTUAL

LIVE OAK STUDIO
Los Feliz, California

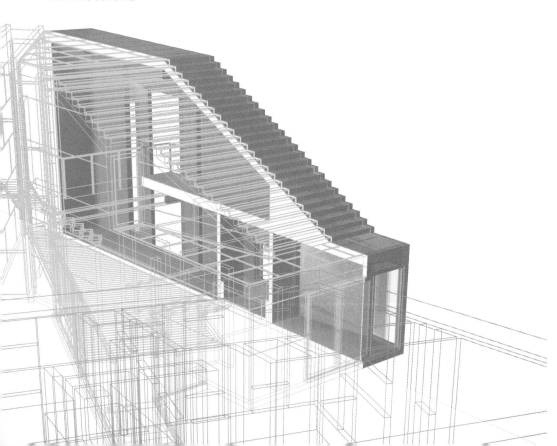

EXPERIENCE
FROM THE ACTUAL
TO THE PERCEPTUAL

The designs of the spaces we inhabit daily have the capacity to shape our lives immeasurably. In our work, a heightened sense of perception is achieved through altering one's experience. The buildings and environments we create are designed to inspire memorable experiences. We achieve this by embedding accommodations for habit and ritual with an acute awareness of the ways in which people occupy their spaces. In our projects, experiences are heightened through the play of geometry, the manipulation of perspective, and the strategic use of specific building materials. A carefully orchestrated experience can result in an enhanced and improved quality of life.

In the Live Oak Studio in Los Feliz, a prescribed path through the building directs the experience of the architecture for the user. One ascends through the building on the way to a rooftop terrace where beautiful panoramic views of Los Angeles are experienced.

In the Milwood project, a more responsive, passive experience occurs via the user's interaction with a body of water located in the middle of the site. The building surrounds the water, towering above and alongside it. The presence and effect of the water are experienced throughout the house.

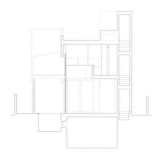

MILWOOD
Venice, California

PERCEPTUAL

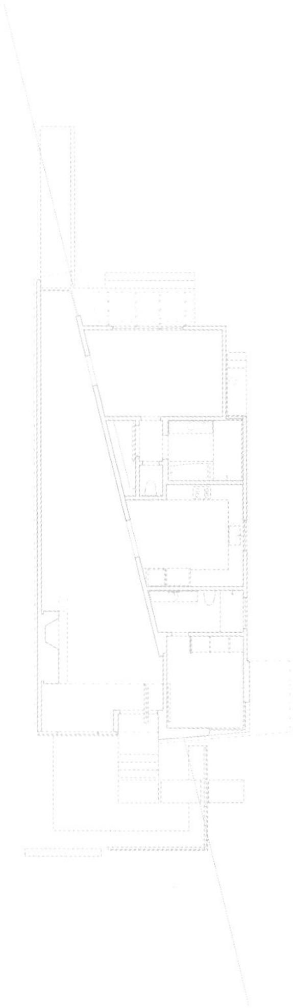

SIMPLE

COLLINS GALLERY
West Hollywood, California

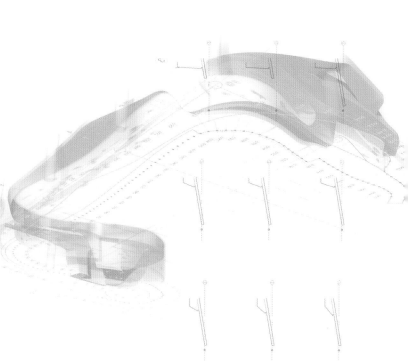

GEOMETRY
FROM THE SIMPLE
TO THE COMPEX

In all of our work, an order or system is imposed—latent, simple, or highly sophisticated.

Our geometric range spans elementary projections, advanced machining, and rapid prototyping. From Euclidean to parametrically produced geometries, the underlying math provides a framework for the unfolding of all architecture. Rules or constraints are inherent within the system, resulting in both order and unexpected outcomes. In our projects, the system is tested and sometimes intentionally broken, creating disturbance and disruption leading to the desired variation.

Earlier work, such as the Collins Gallery, employs a simple geometry where a straight line/wall bisects the building on the diagonal. That simple move creates a forced perspective in both plan and section resulting in a series of unexpected spatial conditions.

Conversely, the Moving Picture Company uses advanced geometry as a means to design, document, and fabricate the complex interior. The technology used in the design process reflects the vision and ideals of the post-production company itself.

MOVING PICTURE COMPANY
Santa Monica, California

COMPLEX

OCEAN FRONT WALK
Venice, California

ANALOG

METHOD
FROM THE ANALOG
TO THE DIGITAL

Our approach employs various methods of producing and representing architecture, each aimed at creating the best resolution
for a project.

When given the opportunity, we exploit the digital to advance
a design and enable the documentation and fabrication of the
advanced geometry. Equally important is the use of less complex
tools such as illustrations and handmade models. Drawing from
both approaches allows us to view a project from numerous
angles, encouraging new ways of seeing. This is inevitably
embodied in the built work, yielding multiple readings of, and
layers of engagement with, the architecture.

Ocean Front Walk on Venice Beach has a straightforward
orthogonal plan and organization. The constraints of the site,
program, and budget drive the method and, ultimately, the
architecture.

Alternatively, the Villa Skhirat for His Highness Sheikh Sultan
bin Zayed Al Nahyan capitalizes on advanced digital processes
for the design, documentation, and the production of the
complex geometry used in the project.

VILLA SKHIRAT
Skhirat, Morocco

DIGITAL

IN TRANSIT

THOM MAYNE

Patrick Tighe, who self describes as having early on "subscribed to the outsider's fantasy," is clearly in transit. For many who start from a perceived position outside, the goal is to arrive, to be inside ... But this, I think, is not what preoccupies Patrick. He seems to be moving from outside to a place that cannot accurately be described as "inside"—perhaps because a notion of inside implies a pinnacle or an end. In analyzing the work and the trajectory of the practice, it is clear that the cultural intransigence of Lowell has been replaced by what so many come west to find: an openness, a sense of experimentation, a freedom to pursue new possibilities. There is none of the gray of Lowell; not in the buildings, not in the imagination, not in the ebullience with which he approaches his projects.

It is interesting that he came to Los Angeles like so many others in our profession, Schindler and Neutra from Europe, Ain and Eames from the East Coast ... all looking for a place that had yet to calcify, that was still open to experimentation and vision and that, even now, still embraces a stance of looking for its own future. For many of the architects who came in the latter half of the 20th century, Los Angeles delivered on its promise and they stayed and worked here, almost exclusively. Now however, something different is happening. Los Angeles has become more than a springboard, it is a veritable hub for young talent of Patrick's generation. Patrick Tighe's work, over the 10 years he's been in practice, has expanded from Los Angeles to include projects in North Africa, the Middle East and Asia. He is the most prolific of his generation of architects with a prodigiousness of output that is an extraordinary testament to the power of desire and talent. What's in evidence in this monograph is a most compelling moment in Tighe's development, where his vast breadth of interests and references are connected to a multiplicity of formal outputs. The diversity of projects in scale, type and complexity range from installations to residential works, from social housing to commercial towers, and seem to demand this diversity and force him to continually access alignments of the formal with broader functional demands of each work.

Whatever it is that brings people to Los Angeles from elsewhere, if they have chosen not to reject the influences of their place of origin, then they are often absorbed and fed creatively by a constant attempt to embrace and resolve dichotomies—much as Patrick does in his work. The East and the West, the right and left, the built and unbuilt, the object and the space in between—are in a constant tension that creates the rudimentary stance from which he, like the city in which he practices, can continually search for himself as he develops his project. And as explicated so well in Stephen Phillips' essay, it is in seeking a resolution to his extant tensions where ideas of ambiguity, distortion, and enigma live that makes it possible to create an authentic and relevant challenge to perception and legibility—and ultimately move toward a new and unique architectural expression.

ENIGMA: DEFAMILIARIZING THE FAMILIAR

STEPHEN PHILLIPS

In his 1965 untitled work, sculptor and theorist Robert Morris presents a simple series of four 3-foot by 3-foot by 2-foot cubes made of fiberglass. Perfectly situated equally and evenly on the floor of a New York gallery, these cubes are seen as four primitives simply set beside one another and appear quite familiar. Morris refers to it as a Gestalt—each single cube appearing part of the whole.

What appears unfamiliar is the forced, distorted, if unreal, perspective of each of the cubes individually and in unity. The familiar object, the primitive, has been defamiliarized through a careful distortion that challenges the viewer to reassess not only the cubic form but the way in which we see in perspective. It is an enigma.

Morris refers to this enigma as a "visual frustration" that challenges our expectations. post-minimalist art of the 1960s aimed to rethink paradigms of minimalist art, pushing toward new ideas in perception, abstraction, figuration, and representation through careful disfiguration of part-to-whole relationships.

Whereas Morris' postmodern work turned towards the post-minimal, Patrick Tighe's contemporary work moves towards the post-digital. Digital architecture of the 1990s to 2000s focused on generating innovative continuous complex-curvilinear forms of tessellated multiplicity through primitive geometries. It posed very discipline-specific, inner-referential, object-oriented designs of pure abstraction. Post-digital architecture, however, has brought a return to the real in an attempt to rethink the language and practice of architecture. It is not a move away from the digital but a hyperdetailed analytical investigation of digital forms and their practices.

Tighe's Tigertail house, for example, rethinks folded topological geometries. Employed ad infinitum since the 1990s by late-deconstructivist architects, folded geometric planes move from ground, to wall, to roof unifying buildings in holistic continuity. For Tighe, the familiar here becomes defamiliar in the over-exaggerated cantilevered roof form that draws our attention toward these folded planes of the house. The hyper-cantilevered roof separates from the overall design, proving an enigma. It is a gesture that challenges our perceptions, creating a looming presence that brings into question the concept of a folded plane. Yet it draws our attention to the site conditions and circulation of the house from the entry, toward the courtyard, and to the centralized pool at the back. For Tighe, the ground becomes a wall, then a roof that gestures toward the sky. The exaggerated roof plane becomes the telltale figure of the Tigertail house, visually legible and rhetorically meaningful. Defamiliarization here reveals the concept/idea of the design. It poses the place where one is to look to understand Tighe's architecture.

We see this same form of disfiguration in Tighe's Jacobs Subterranean house design, where the

"up and down" staircase performs a similarly familiar postmodern trope. Robert Venturi, back in 1964, originally rethought the paradigm of a "stair" by questioning the limits, if not the very notion, of what a stair was and could be. This was posited through an uncomfortable, if not awkward, shift in the rise, run, and path of a stair. Tighe here designs a similarly challenging stair that rises and falls, and goes up and goes down, rethinking the history of the grand overtly symmetrical redundancy of the Beaux-Arts stair. The added shift in the wall plane of the Jacobs Subterranean house is reminiscent of the interior spaces of Robert Weine's 1920 film *The Cabinet of Dr. Caligari*, alongside the elongated stair treads of architect Alvar Aalto's famous stair in the Villa Mairea House.

Tighe engages in a discourse of familiarity: the proverbial Beaux-Arts stair, the expressionist stair, the modernist stair, the postmodernist stair, as wells as the deconstructivist stair, all at once. This historic discourse helps us to rethink the very notion of a stair. Through a few playful gestures and moves of distortion, disfigurement, and deconstruction, it brings to attention the habitual familiarity of the stair and how a stair may be used.

This playful disfiguring and reconfiguring of a familiar trope in architecture—whether it is a stair in the Jacobs Subterranean house, the corner façade treatment of the La Brea Housing design, the guard rail of the Sierra Bonita Mixed-Use Affordable Housing project, or in the stair at one of his most accomplished designs, the Montee Karp residence—are linguistic signs that point toward valued meaning within Tighe's projects. They are specific tectonic elements that become separated from the overall design visually and architecturally through enigmatic juxtapositions. They draw our attention to specific design elements that, upon close analysis, reveal cultural engagement with modern and contemporary design discourses, as well as ideas about site, program, and linguistic practices in architecture.

The Montee Karp house is a terrific example of Tighe's expertise. Presented as a white, pristine crystalline form, the house takes on the familiar image of a pitched-roof house (which it was before the remodel), alongside very contemporary formal strategies that disfigure primitive monolithic geometries. This is not a unique practice but a very familiar one. Of interest to contemporary post-digital artists and architects alike during the past decade—primitive vocabularies, entirely embedded in the software we use (Maya/Rhino), can be employed through additive and subtractive box-modeling Boolean techniques to generate innovative form. Unlike complex curvilinear surfaces generated through Nurbs-modeling techniques, box modeling can provide us with an architecture of developable surfaces that, if dynamic and computer-generated, are also quite easy to fabricate and build. Primitive geometric forms are at once monolithic, generating a complete whole, while at the same time readily disfigured.

Box modeling in architecture has become quite familiar. Disruptions, breaks, awkward gestures, and discontinuous moments within such vocabularies produce unfamiliar territories: the distorted pivoting door, the thin-perspective-corner-strip window, the shallow-monolithic-chamfered sink, the hovering-garage portico. These elements that stand out from the overall monolithic abstract Gestalt figure are important signs. Similar to what Roland Barthes argues in his famous essay "The Third Meaning." These disfiguring elements call our attention, suggesting that the viewer imagine new forms of meaning—for example, the way the new roof of the addition to the Montee Karp house pitches to form part of a solid that wraps around the original house. At once, it unifies with the original house, forming a Gestalt between old and new, but then separates from it with distorted angularity. It suggests the rethinking of the original house itself.

The contemporary house is not entirely different from the traditional house. Similar to where the Vanna Venturi façade explored traditional elements of the familiar by reconfiguring, reclaiming, and reconstituting them within a new postmodern vocabulary—contemporary post-digital architecture uses digital practices to rethink the elements of contemporary building design. Akin to the deconstructivists of the 1960s to 1980s, we have recently begun to utilize shifts in perspective, distortions in surface pattern, and a wide range of disfigurements in rhetorically meaningful ways to generate intelligent design practices.

These are the questions posed in Tighe's most recent works, the West Cork Arts Center, the Taichung Fine Arts Museum and Library, and Twin. The distortion of the primitive monolith sophisticatedly draws focus and attention to the main concept of each design. The West Cork Arts Center presents a tubular architecture, for example, reminiscent of early extruded digital design vocabularies with a carefully crafted set of end conditions—one crude and simply cut (the familiar) and the other deconstructed and enigmatic (the unfamiliar). Tighe takes the proverbial corner window to a new extreme linguistic sensibility. Here, the corner-glazed-window-wall-floor relationship becomes a unique configuration, one inseparable element that is illusionary, visually frustrating, and conceptually challenging. We are inspired to ask ourselves what would it feel like to walk on a glass floor—one that is not a floor per se but a window that is not a window but also a wall.

More provocative than simply walking across a modern glass cube or simple cast-glass floor, you are able to move in your mind's eye from a solid floor to walking upon a window. The corner window is still represented as a window. It still reads linguistically as a window. But it is now also becoming a floor. It is at once a floor while at the same time part of a corner window assembly. These part-whole relationships are rhetorical, representational, and in that simple move, what we might call neo-postmodern.

With the return to linguistic meaning in architecture, as demonstrated by the West Cork Arts Center, the Taichung Fine Arts Museum and Library brings forward the return of the digitally designed complex curvilinear, continuous smooth forms of the 1990s. Wall, floor, and roof, as Frederick Kiesler had originally imagined it best in the Endless House of the 1960s, has here returned with a glitch. It is now cut, cracked, broken, ruptured. The distortion in the holistic form along the center of the roof, through to the window, draws our focus and attention. The continuous forms are of course very familiar, but the cut that breaks the system is not. It combines the skylight and window, adding tension to the design. Tension is a moment held open by the unease of incompletion, where anticipation and the desire for completion is left unfulfilled and unresolved.

The cut draws our interest toward a centralizing courtyard and organizational strategy of the plan. This is the critical mark of this design, and if here, it is somewhat unresolved, the same idea is picked up again in the Twin. The cut is severe, revealing the circulation and organizational strategy of the building containing the main stair. The cut in the overall continuous surface of the distorted primitive forms of the house defines the path of entry that slips between the outer skin of the wall, and reappears as apertures for rear balconies and other windows.

The skin becomes the main figure in this design, which is bent, shaped, and chamfered around the interior space of each unit. The overall figure, if distorted, becoming again quite familiar—where the tectonic elements of stair, window, skylight, and balcony all become the discursive and descriptive aspects of the house. The architectural elements formulate a language that communicate and speak about the design. When learning to read a building, one must look to the unfamiliar, and in the case perhaps of the Twin becoming all too familiar, we might ask the designer to challenge us even more.

Significantly, architecture does not need to search outside itself to become linguistic. It does not need to mimic or reconfigure outmoded, nostalgic, or antiquated figures from past vocabularies to become intelligent and legible. It can and arguably should employ a contemporary vocabulary in new and innovative ways to engage in a discussion of cultural value and meaningful dialogue. Great architects construct their own architectural language. And to have a language that is relevant and discursive, it must speak to ever-evolving contemporary issues. Although it is important to share common ground with one's peers for architecture to engage in discourse and debate, once an architect's language becomes readily understood, complete, and whole within itself (i.e. too familiar), it becomes normal, habitual, unconscious, and boring.

For Robert Morris, a 64-sided figure may be difficult to comprehend in its entirety at first, but once its regularity is identified, it becomes whole and

with that dismissed as understood. Irregularity thereby becomes very important to a designer. It can particularize a specific quality, drawing attention to what is different. Taken to the extreme however, a complex crystalline form, for example, can subvert any effort to comprehend the whole, creating weak Gestalts as they cannot be readily comprehended. They remain irrelevant and undecipherable in parts. A building form too complex that never forms a Gestalt is unresolvable and arguably lacks cohesion of design. A building form, sleek, synthetic, and complete, becomes a one-liner, simplistic, and readily dismissed.

Gaming part-whole relationships is thereby very important to developing valued subject-object relationships. Ambiguity, enigma, irregularity, distortion, discontinuity, and unfamiliarity all challenge monolithic Gestalt shapes, forms, and patterns. They generate curiosity and intensity. They frustrate visual perception and legibility. The tension generated between an overall design, pattern, or form—a Gestalt against moments of rupture and fragmentation—is paramount to understanding a type of contemporary formalism rooted in post-minimalist and postmodern interests of the 1960s. Paired with well-developed retooling and rethinking, it is what we might call the deconstructivist twist.

A HOUSE DIVIDED

COLLINS GALLERY

WEST HOLLYWOOD,
CALIFORNIA

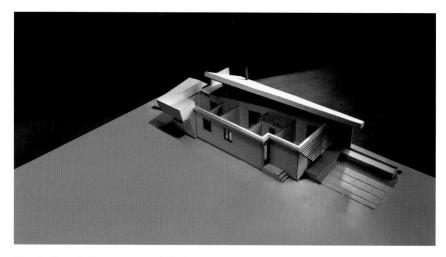

STATUS: BUILT 2002
SITE: 4,000 SQ.FT.
AREA: 2,100 SQ.FT.
TYPE: RESIDENTIAL /
GALLERY
PROGRAM: SINGLE FAMILY
DWELLING / EXHIBITION
SPACE
OWNER: MICHAEL COLLINS

SIMPLE

The Collins Gallery—a remodel of a tract house in the West Hollywood Arts District—bridges the residents' domestic needs with their requirements as art dealers. The challenge was to create a spacious gallery area and residence within a relatively small building envelope. Despite substandard construction and lack of architectural significance, the original building was subject to city regulations. Square footage and the footprint of existing homes needed to be maintained, and a minimum of 50 percent of the existing walls had to remain intact. The scale-appropriate response maintains harmony with neighboring buildings.

The manipulation of a simple geometry creates a play on perceptions. A new load-bearing wall bisects the building on the diagonal, creating two distinct zones, differentiating the gallery from the residence. With this one simple move, the space appears to increase in size dramatically. The articulation of materials further reinforces the idea of separate public and private zones. The zinc-clad façade is a heavy, strong piece that designates the residence. The 5-foot-wide, steel-framed, glass pivot door provides a grand entry. Opposing programs coexist.

The gallery's roof plane is lifted to allow for the penetration of natural light, through the clerestory, the primary light source. It makes windows optional, while maximizing wall surface for the display of art. The laminated, opaque glass of the storefront curtain wall allows northern light to filter into the gallery. Another perspective was achieved within the gallery by tapering it, in both plan and section, out to the garden courtyard. A 20-foot-long reflecting pool extends the gallery floor plane, pushing the space beyond the building envelope. The fireplace, a continuation of the tilted roof plane, functions as an easel for viewing art.

SIMPLE

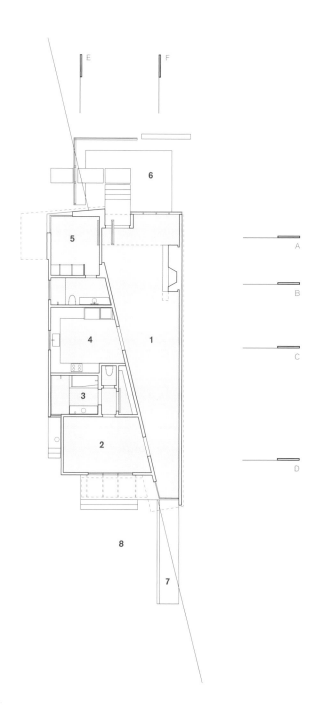

1. GALLERY **2.** MASTER BEDROOM **3.** MASTER BATHROOM **4.** KITCHEN **5.** DEN **6.** COURTYARD
7. REFLECTING POOL **8.** COURTYARD

PERCEPTUAL

SIMPLE

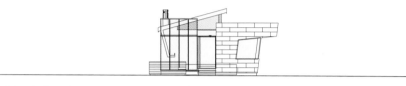

NORTH ELEVATION

SOUTH ELEVATION

WEST ELEVATION

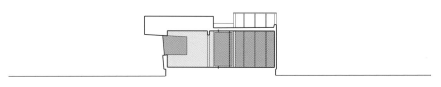

SECTION A

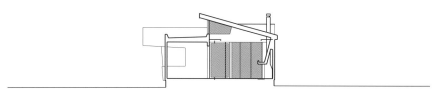

SECTION B

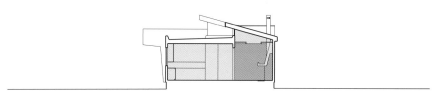

SECTION C

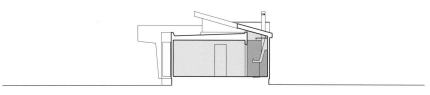

SECTION D

SIMPLE

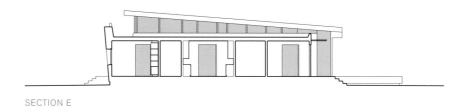

SECTION E

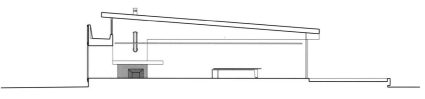

SECTION F

SIMPLE

PERCEPTUAL

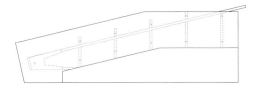

TOP

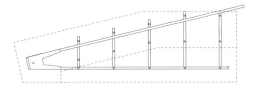

PLAN

SIDE ELEVATION

SIMPLE

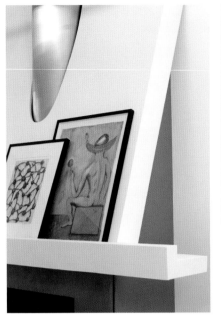

UP THE DOWN STAIRCASE

JACOBS SUBTERRANEAN

SHERMAN OAKS,
CALIFORNIA

SIMPLE

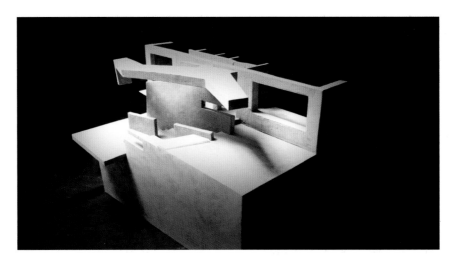

STATUS: BUILT 2002
SITE: 12,000 SQ.FT.
AREA: 3,400 SQ.FT.
TYPE: GALLERY
PROGRAM: EXHIBITION
SPACE
OWNER: RAY AND SILVIA
JACOBS

This project in Sherman Oaks, California, began with a 1,200-square-foot excavation carved out of seemingly uninhabitable space beneath an existing post-and-beam residence on a hillside site. The terraced solution satisfies strict code requirements that inhibit altering the existing structure. The new extension joins the living quarters above to the garden below, creating a contemporary escape, refuge, and oasis under the existing home. Angled walls, multiple floor planes, and manipulated white wall planes provide a theatrical backdrop for our client's art collection.

The large gesture of the cascading stair connects all the floors of the multitiered space, creating a unified whole. The stair, wider toward the center and narrower at both ends, creates a forced perspective. Experientially, this results in altered perceptions as one ascends or descends the stair, with the angled wall transforming into a soffit overhead. The floating form reinforces movement through the space and contains the mechanical and sound systems.

The experiences of descending and ascending the new space intensify and amalgamate the transition between the old and new elements of the home. The kitchenette is tucked beneath the shower. All levels and the landscape beyond are visible from the entertainment room. 12-foot-high sliding glass doors open to the heavily wooded garden. Ceiling heights vary at each level reaching a maximum height of 16 feet at the music room. The bathroom, adjacent to the grand stair and central to all levels, has laminated opaque glass walls. A horizontal plane of stainless steel anchors the lavatory, penetrating the glass wall and becoming a focal point at the hallway. When illuminated, the bathing chamber is omnipresent and the silhouette of the activity within is revealed. The space underneath the home, typically considered unfit for traditional domestic use, has been transformed into a peaceful, personal sanctuary.

PERCEPTUAL

SIMPLE

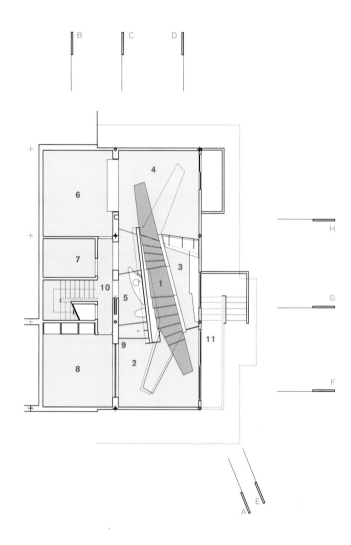

1. STAIR 2. MUSIC ROOM 3. OFFICE 4. GALLERY 5. BATHROOM 6. BEDROOM 7. LAUNDRY
8. TV ROOM 9. KITCHENETTE 10. UP TO RESIDENCE 11. DOWN TO GARDEN

FLOOR PLAN

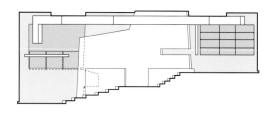

SECTION A

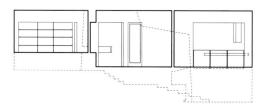

SECTION B

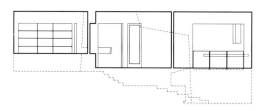

SECTION C

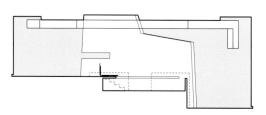

SECTION D

SIMPLE

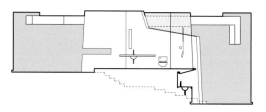

SECTION E

SECTIONS

A ROOM OF ONE'S OWN

ASHCROFT WRITER'S STUDIO

WEST HOLLYWOOD,
CALIFORNIA

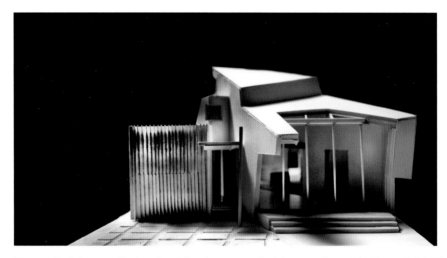

STATUS: BUILT 2006
SITE: 4,200 SQ.FT.
AREA: 2,700 SQ.FT.
TYPE: RESIDENTIAL
PROGRAM: SINGLE FAMILY
DWELLING
OWNER: RICK ZBUR

The project for a writer's retreat is at once central to and secluded from Los Angeles. It is sited in proximity to the Pacific Design Center. The massing and form of the new building reference the nearby iconic Pelli monoliths.

The 2,700-square-foot live-work space consists of a double-height volume tapering in plan to create a forced perspective and then opening out toward the adjacent gardens, exaggerating the scale of the gardens. Northern light filters through the clerestory window above, washing the cascading planes of the interior ceiling-scape with a soft, natural light.

The folded roof descends toward and opens up at the street where a transition exists between the privacy of the building and the public space, including West Hollywood passersby. This idea of public versus private is key to the design of the project.

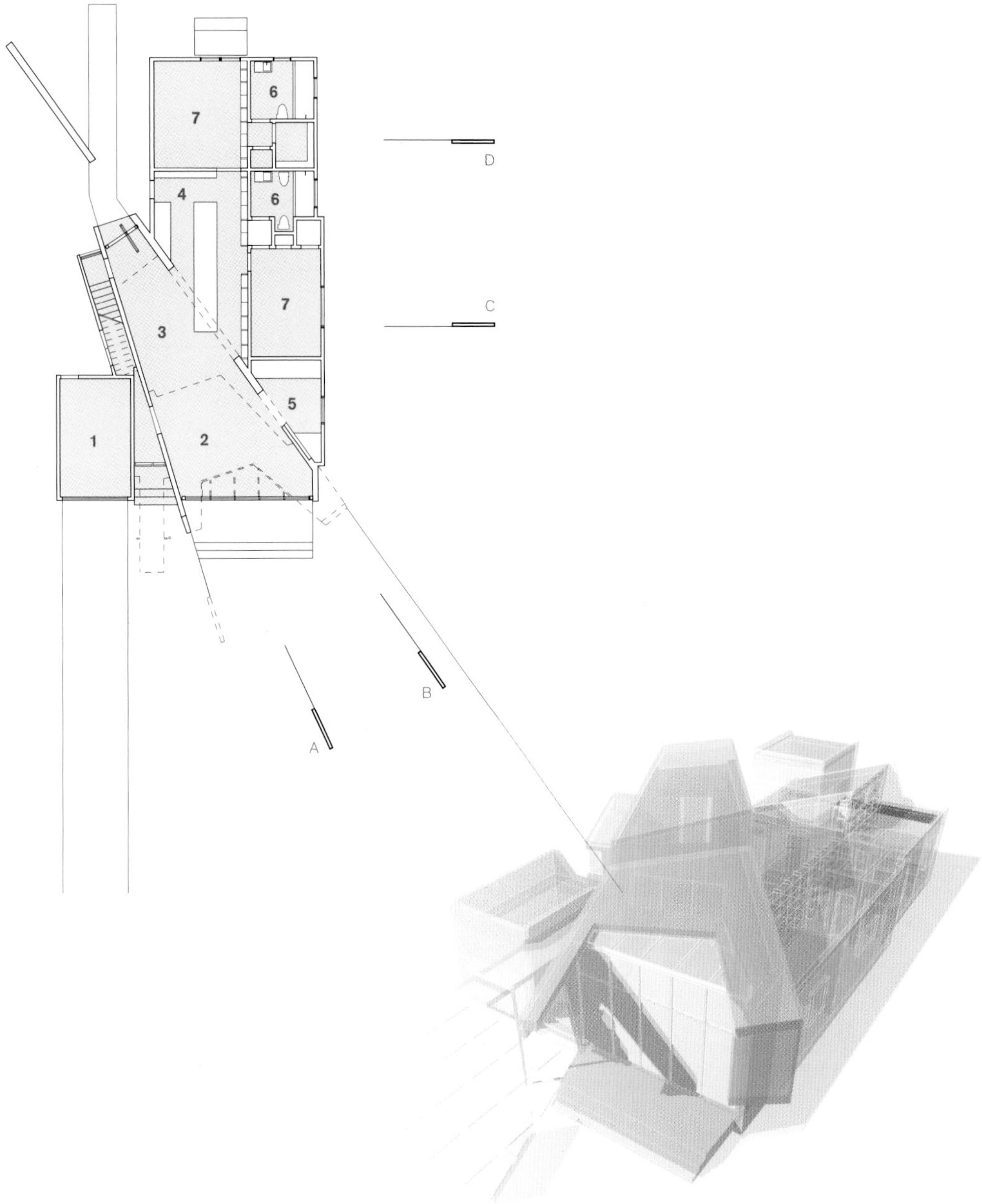

D

C

B

A

1. GARAGE **2.** LIVING ROOM **3.** DINING ROOM **4.** KITCHEN **5.** STUDY **6.** BATHROOM **7.** BEDROOM

ANALOG

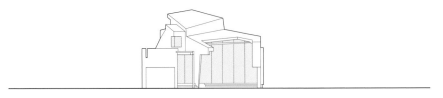

SOUTH ELEVATION

WEST ELEVATION

NORTH ELEVATION

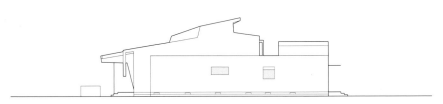

EAST ELEVATION

ELEVATIONS

LE MÉPRIS / LOS FELIZ

LIVE OAK STUDIO

LOS FELIZ, CALIFORNIA

ACTUAL

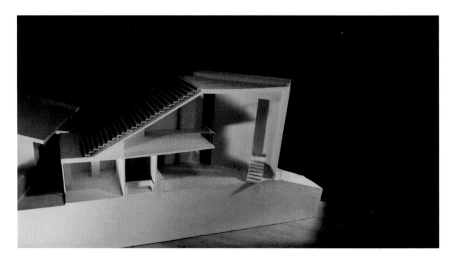

STATUS: BUILT 2004
SITE: 14,000 SQ.FT.
AREA: 3,600 SQ.FT.
TYPE: ARTIST'S STUDIO
PROGRAM: SINGLE FAMILY
DWELLING / PAINTER'S
STUDIO
OWNER: STEVEN
WERNDORF

At the intersection of two winding streets in the Hollywood Hills is a wedge-shaped building that follows the landscape contours, with massing that mimics its mountainous surroundings. The project is strategically placed on the site, so it is not in competition with the adjacent Wallace Neff house. The new building compliments the existing structure by using a similar palette of materials. From the parcel, the dominant view is of the Griffith Observatory. The omnipresent Hollywood sign is above, and the Los Angeles cityscape is in the distance.

Our film industry client imagined a space similar to a scene in the Godard film, Le Mépris, where Brigitte Bardot descends the exterior stair of the Casa Malaparte on the island of Capri. That image was the starting point for design. The program consists of a painting studio, master bedroom suite, and a

loft. It intentionally leads people through a variety of experiences as they ascend the space. One perceives the power of the site through a series of framed views arranged along the prescribed route. Glimpses of what lies beyond build anticipation.

The double-height space serves as a painter's studio, partially lit by indirect light filtering in from the stairwell shaft. An oversized, 20-foot-tall sliding door opens to a direct view of the observatory. From the studio, one may continue up to the loft. The stairwell is sandwiched between two walls, with storefront glazing at either end and a view of the site's mature trees. The second level opens to a roof deck with a grand exterior stair of precast concrete planks. There are extraordinary views from the roof terrace. The plateau is a stage set, with the Hollywood Hills and the major icons of Los Angeles forming the background.

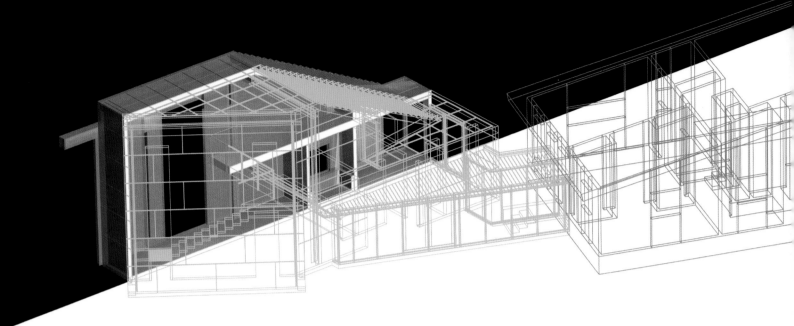

ACTUAL

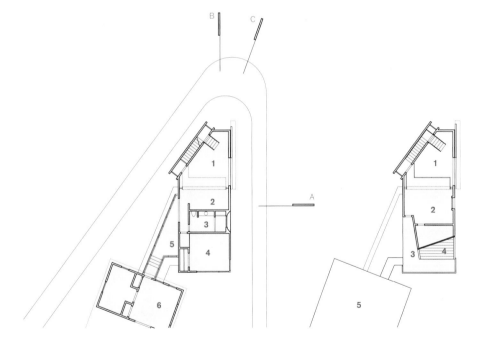

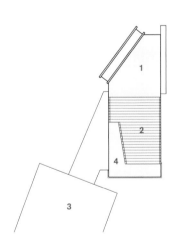

GROUND LEVEL
1. STUDIO 2. KITCHEN 3. BATHROOM
4. BEDROOM 5. GALLERY 6. EXISTING
BUILDING

LOFT LEVEL
1. OPEN TO STUDIO BELOW 2. LOFT
3. LOWER ROOF TERRACE 4. STAIRS TO
ROOF TERRACE 5. EXISTING BUILDING

ROOF
1. ROOF TERRACE 2. STAIRS UP TO ROOF
TERRACE 3. LOWER ROOF TERRACE
4. EXISTING BUILDING

ACTUAL

ACTUAL

EAST ELEVATION

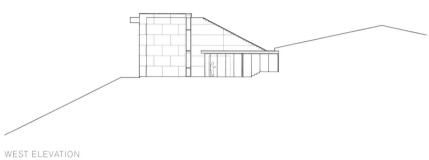

WEST ELEVATION

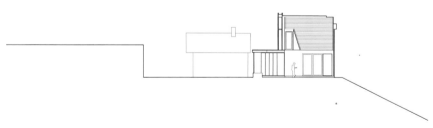

SOUTH ELEVATION

ELEVATIONS

ACTUAL

SUBURBAN SPRAWL

REDONDO BEACH HOUSE

REDONDO BEACH,
CALIFORNIA

NATURAL

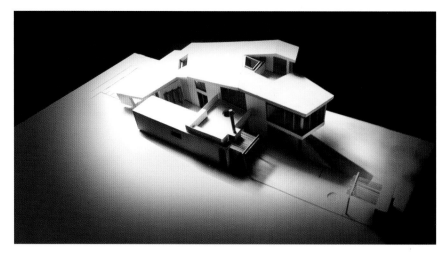

STATUS: BUILT 2006
SITE: 6,000 SQ.FT.
AREA: 3,500 SQ.FT.
TYPE: RESIDENTIAL
PROGRAM: SINGLE FAMILY
DWELLING
OWNER: GORDON DONLOU

The 3,500-square-foot residence in Redondo Beach, California is located a half mile from the Pacific Ocean. The design comprises a massing of faceted volumes surrounding a central courtyard. The building is grounded at the suburban neighborhood condition, and a larger, more expressive volume rises to the west to maximize views to the ocean and the city. The scale of the neighborhood is preserved by single-story massing at the street. There are other contrasts in the project, such as a traditional rectilinear and trapezoidal floor plan, both set on one side of the home at ground level.

The two building volumes intertwine, creating the central courtyard where glass walls open onto an outdoor room. This courtyard garden is the focus of all activity and also functions as the main entry. The courtyard typology is exploited, turning the house inside-out and focusing the energy inward, creating a personal refuge.

The east-west axis is maintained as the two entities circumscribe the courtyard. Folded metal roof planes conceal multiple exterior decks. The roof surface becomes the façade, breaking down the scale of the building, while simultaneously offering a smooth transition from one level to the next. The master bedroom appears to float above the swimmers' pool. The body of water has a strong visual and aural connection to the building, and its effects are experienced throughout the house, referencing proximity to the ocean.

NATURAL

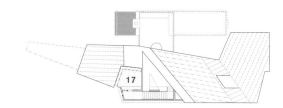

THIRD LEVEL

SECOND LEVEL

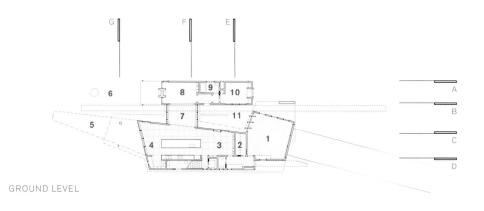

GROUND LEVEL

1. GARAGE 2. LAUNDRY ROOM 3. DEN 4. KITCHEN 5. POOL 6. GARDEN 7. DINING ROOM
8. LIVING ROOM 9. BATHROOM 10. STUDY 11. COURTYARD 12. TERRACE 13. BEDROOM
14. MASTER BATHROOM 15. MASTER BEDROOM 16. ROOF TERRACE 17. UPPER ROOF DECK

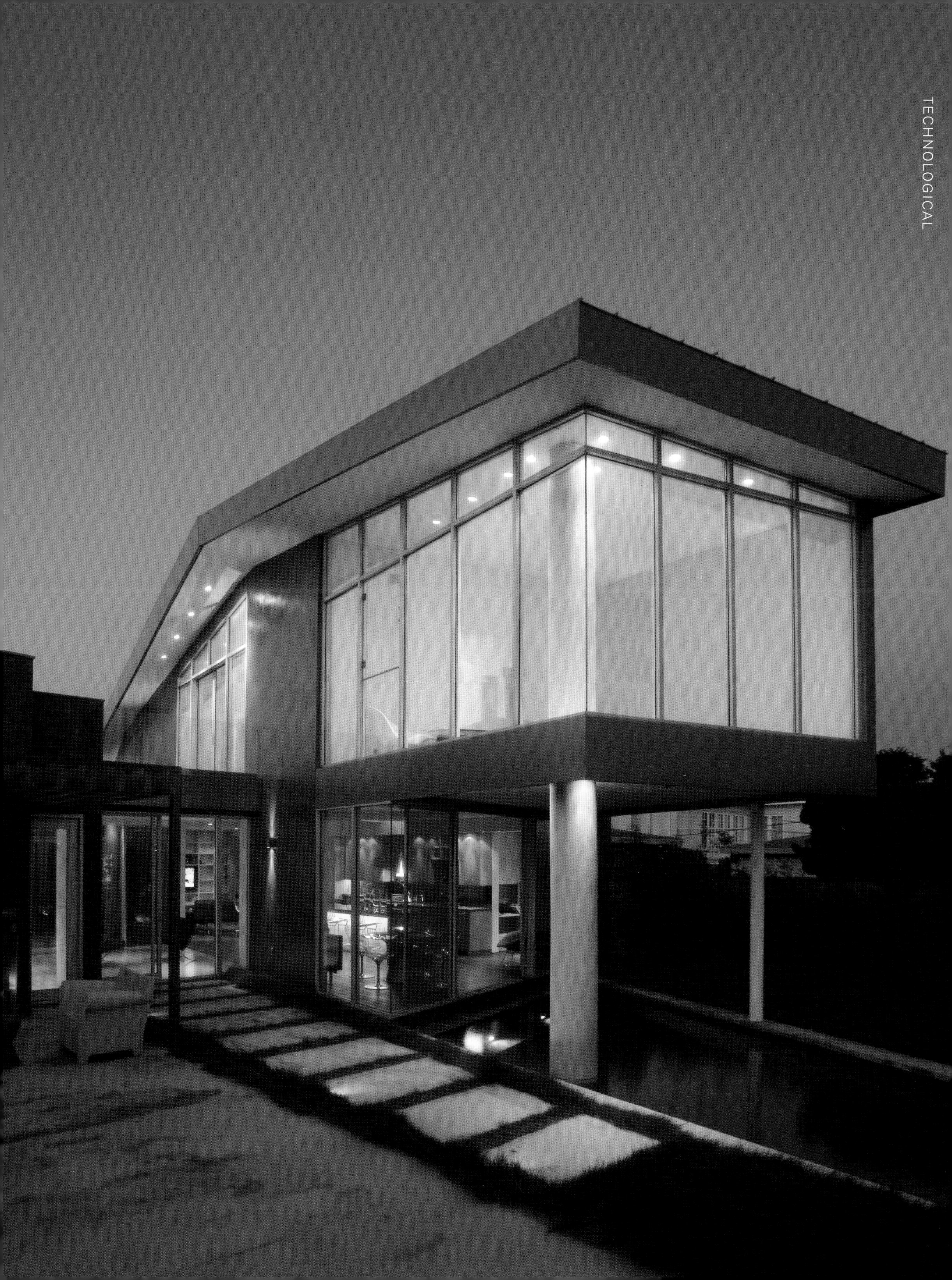

NATURAL

EAST ELEVATION

NORTH ELEVATION

SOUTH ELEVATION

WEST ELEVATION

ELEVATIONS

NATURAL

SECTION A

SECTION B

SECTION C

SECTION D

ON THE BOARDWALK

OCEAN FRONT WALK

VENICE BEACH,
CALIFORNIA

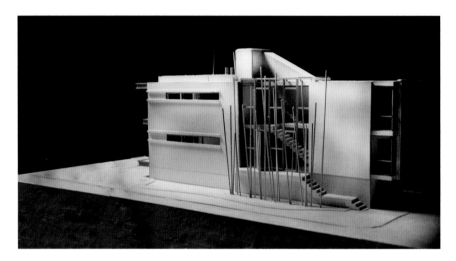

STATUS: BUILT 2008
SITE: 4,000 SQ.FT.
AREA: 3,600 SQ.FT.
TYPE: RESIDENTIAL
PROGRAM: SINGLE FAMILY
DWELLING
OWNER: FARID KIA

The 3,600-square-foot residence occupies a tight corner lot along the boardwalk in Venice, California. The site itself is only 25 feet by 100 feet and is located on a very public walk street. The design investigates the interplay between public and private with the ultimate goal of keeping the residence as open as possible, while simultaneously retaining some semblance of privacy.

A double-height atrium space provides entry into the building. A heavy concrete base with a matte foundation visually anchors it to the site. Three steel moment frames provide the primary structural framework and also allow full transparency at the ocean side of the residence. An interior wall diagonally bisects the narrow building longitudinally at an angle, creating a forced perspective, opening the 20-foot by 90-foot space wider toward the Pacific Ocean, giving the illusion of a much larger interior area. The utilities are hidden within the service core.

The southern elevation is highly visible from the beach. The long façade is divided into three distinct zones. Durable, weather-resistant materials consisting of zinc, cement fiberboard, and plaster cover the surface. A rooftop deck provides panoramic views of the coast. A solar canopy, rooftop garden, and other sustainable building systems and materials are integral to the design.

The public aspect is resolved through the degree of transparency built into the design, since the house is intended for the public and the residents to be on display—to see and to be seen. The fully glazed southwest façade allows unobstructed views of the ocean early in the morning and in the evening. Throughout the day, one can observe the best that Venice beach life has to offer.

ANALOG

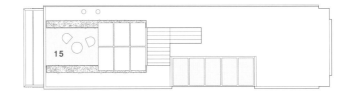

ROOF

SECOND LEVEL

FIRST LEVEL

SUBTERRANEAN LEVEL

1. PAINTER'S STUDIO 2. LAUNDRY ROOM 3. GARAGE 4. ENTRANCE 5. KITCHEN 6. DINING
ROOM 7. POWDER ROOM 8. LIVING ROOM 9. DECK 10. BEDROOM 11. MASTER BEDROOM
12. MASTER BATHROOM 13. CLOSET 14. BATHROOM 15. ROOF TERRACE

ANALOG

FLOOR PLANS

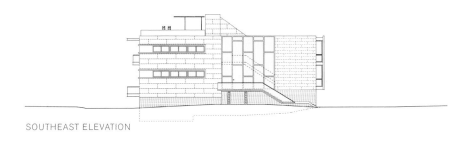

SOUTHEAST ELEVATION

SOUTHWEST ELEVATION

NORTHWEST ELEVATION

NORTHEAST ELEVATION

ELEVATIONS

MANUFACTURED

FOLDED TOPO

TIGERTAIL

BRENTWOOD,
CALIFORNIA

STATUS: BUILT 2008
SITE: 28,000 SQ.FT.
AREA: 3,200 SQ.FT.
TYPE: RESIDENTIAL
PROGRAM: SINGLE FAMILY
DWELLING
OWNER: DR. HUGH
MACDONALD

The 3,200-square-foot residence, located in the Crestwood Hills neighborhood of Brentwood, California, is a postwar development of modest mid-century homes. It consists of a new two-story building integrated with the existing residence. The architecture builds upon the original intent of the pioneers of progressive development, such as A. Quincy Jones. Pragmatic aspects of the topography and more complex three-dimensional manipulations of form merge to respect but not mimic the site; however, various site conditions do inform the design.

The residence is kept low, matching the scale of the neighboring homes along the street. The unusual geometry of the second-story volume results from existing conditions and setback regulations. Openings for views work with and against solid walls for shear

and privacy, defining the building envelope. A series of bent, steel moment frames noticeably straddle the existing one-story structure. Folded roof and wall planes, sheathed in interlocking metal panels, are an extension of the rolling topography of the hillside site. The wood-clad interior dissolves the distinctions between walls, ceiling, and floor. Views are framed by glass walls throughout, as the building projects outward to the city, the ocean, and the neighboring Getty Center in the distance.

The project began with a modest home, typical of others in the neighborhood, built in the same period. The intervention of the contemporary addition results in a striking contrast through use of folded planes, metal panels, and forms and materials representative of the landscape.

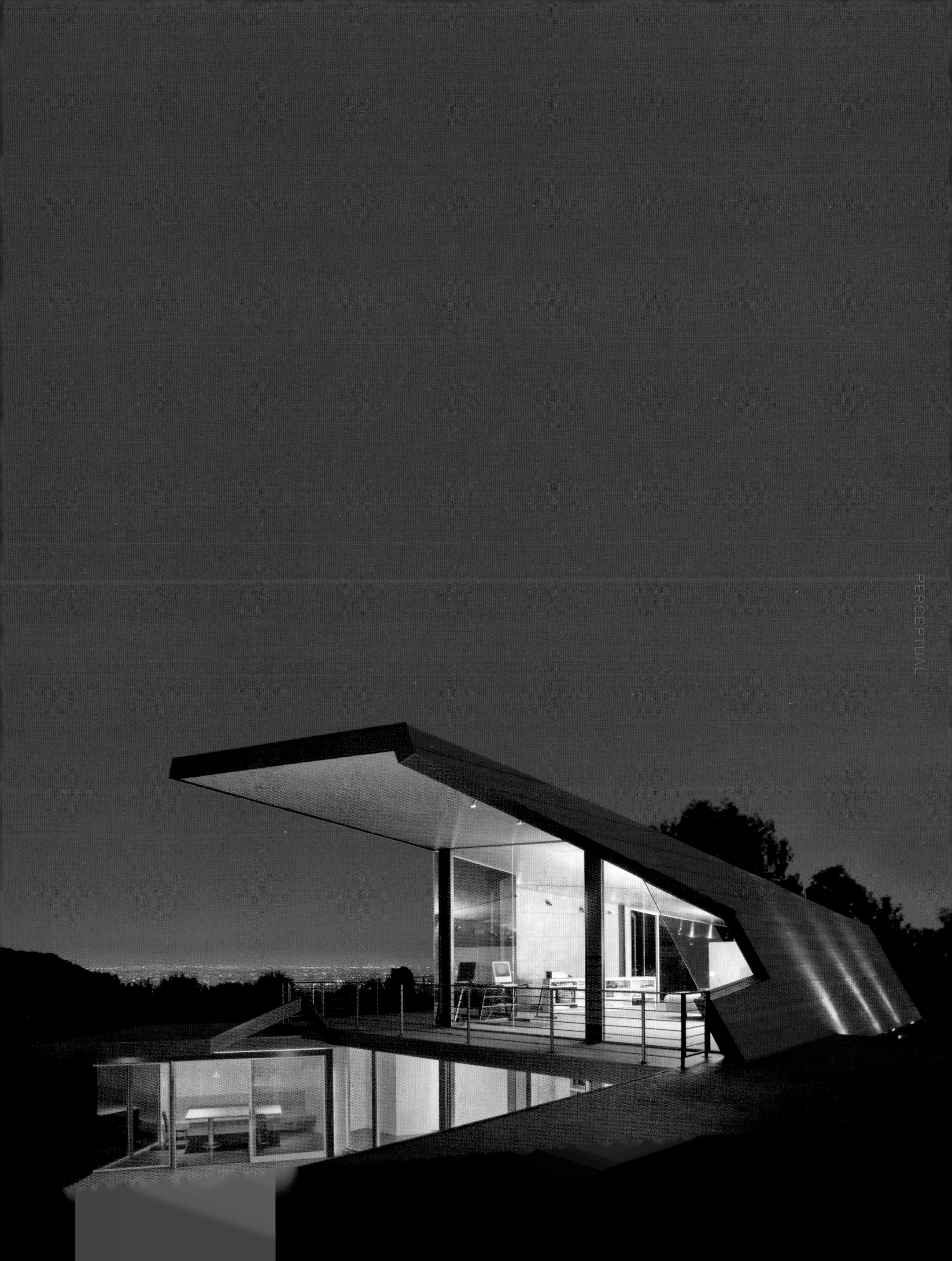

MANUFACTURED

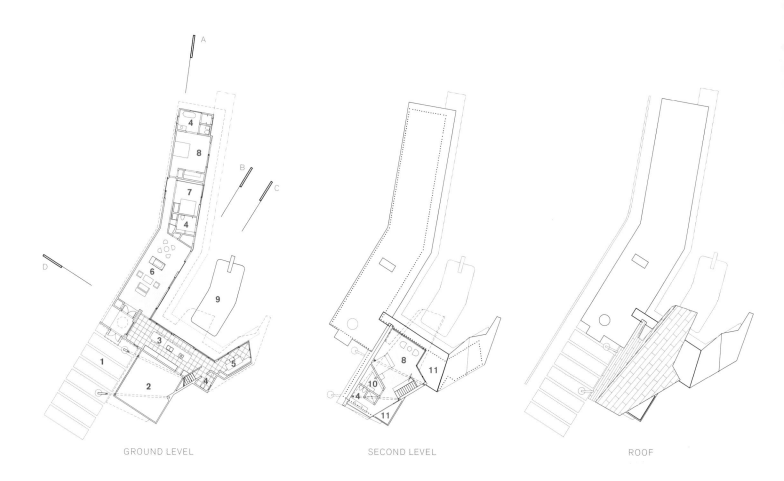

GROUND LEVEL   SECOND LEVEL   ROOF

1. ENTRANCE 2. GARAGE 3. KITCHEN 4. BATHROOM 5. DEN 6. LIVING ROOM 7. MEDIA ROOM
8. BEDROOM 9. POOL 10. CLOSET 11. DECK

FLOOR PLANS

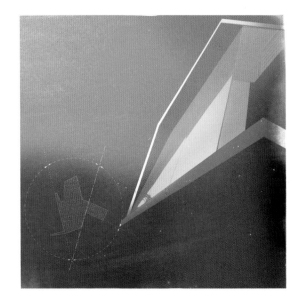

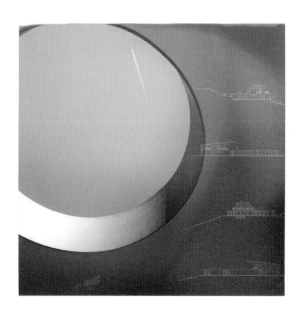

MANUFACTURED

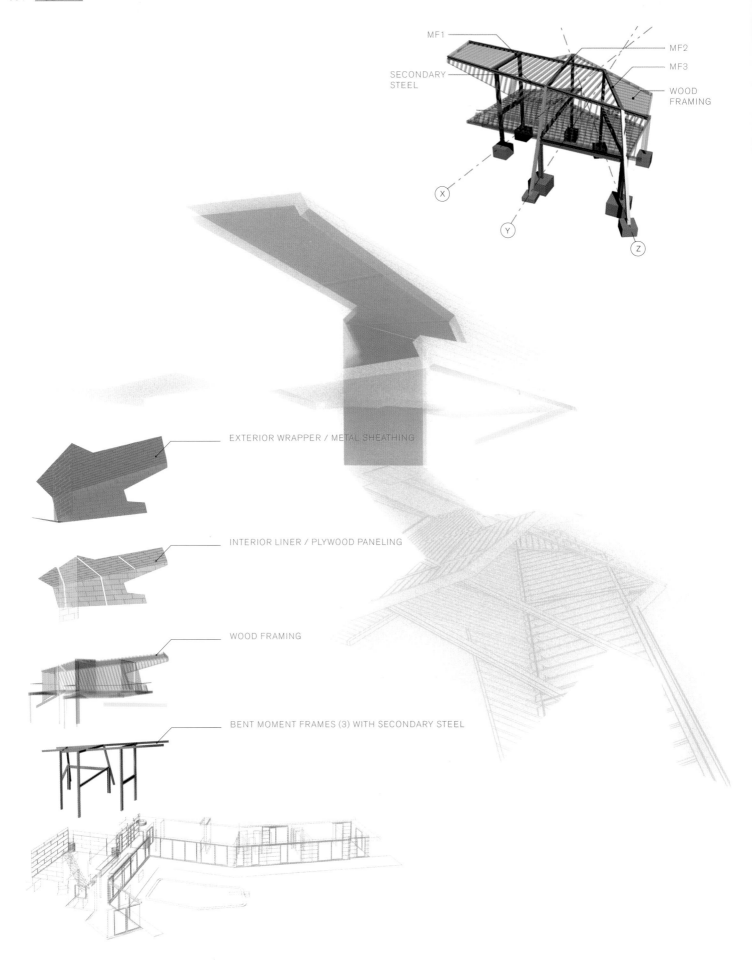

MF1

MF2

MF3

SECONDARY
STEEL

WOOD
FRAMING

X

Y

Z

EXTERIOR WRAPPER / METAL SHEATHING

INTERIOR LINER / PLYWOOD PANELING

WOOD FRAMING

BENT MOMENT FRAMES (3) WITH SECONDARY STEEL

BUILDING COMPONENTS / STRUCTURAL DIAGRAM

MANUFACTURED

MANUFACTURED

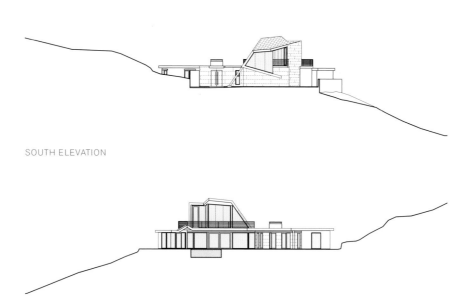

SOUTH ELEVATION

NORTH ELEVATION

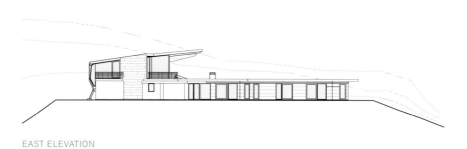

EAST ELEVATION

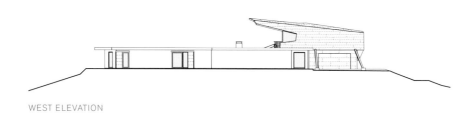

WEST ELEVATION

ELEVATIONS

PERCEPTUAL

MANUFACTURED

FIR CLAD

BLACK BOX

SANTA MONICA,
CALIFORNIA

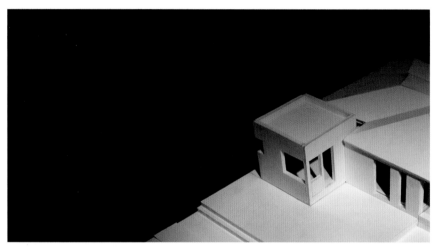

STATUS: BUILT 2005
SITE: 5,000 SQ.FT.
AREA: 1,600 SQ.FT.
TYPE: RESIDENTIAL
PROGRAM: SINGLE FAMILY
DWELLING
OWNER: PRIVATE

The Black Box is designed in the Scandinavian tradition with an earthy palette of natural materials. The supple dark volume consisting of a 14-foot cube provides a contrasting backdrop for the existing magnolia blossoms and white birch branches on site. Due to the modest scale of the building, the volumetric design is a study in restraint.

The versatile interior functions as a living, sleeping, and work area. As a consequence of its relatively small size, livable space is at a premium. Orthogonal geometry, economy of means, and precise proportions work in tandem to maximize space. To accommodate multiple functions, built-ins are employed as key elements of the design.

Building components were selected from those readily available or recycled. The building envelope is created from vertical wood siding mounted over asphalt roof shingles. The wood siding is protected with a sooty, burnt tar stain. The brooding, dark exterior and the blonde interior stand in stark contrast to one another. Interior surfaces are a series of horizontal bands comprising wood applications. The shifting horizontal zones define the penetrations in the building and accommodate built-in amenities. The siding and deck are made of recycled wood. Windows are made with steel angles, and perforated steel screens enclose the building for privacy.

MANUFACTURED

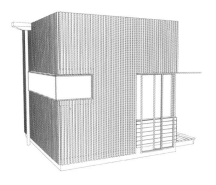

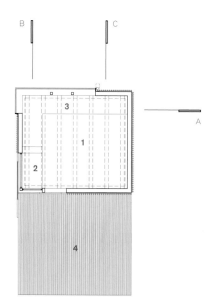

1. LIVING SPACE **2.** DESK **3.** BUILT-IN SEATING **4.** TERRACE

MANUFACTURED

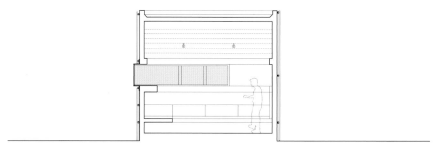

SECTION A

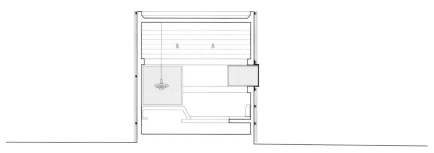

SECTION B

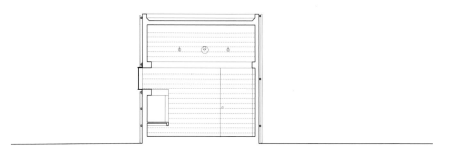

SECTION C

SECTIONS

NATURAL

HOME ON THE RANGE

TRAHAN RANCH

AUSTIN, TEXAS

STATUS: BUILT 2007
SITE: 48,000 SQ.FT.
AREA: 3,800 SQ.FT.
TYPE: RESIDENTIAL
PROGRAM: SINGLE FAMILY
DWELLING
OWNER: JOHN TRAHAN

The 3,800-square-foot residential project in the heart of Texas Hill Country is on a 14-acre sloping site with native oaks, natural springs, and unobstructed views. The plan is a direct response to the site conditions, organized to experience the rugged characteristics of the indigenous landscape. The buildings are nestled into the brow of the hill—a position that offers 260-degree panoramic views—with an unassuming appearance when seen from a distance.

The architecture incorporates a series of counterpoints, including heavy and light, open and closed, and contemporary and vernacular. The steel frame structure is a kit of parts prefabricated in a shop and erected on site. The steel pieces attach to a series of exposed, board-formed, reinforced concrete pylons that are vertical extensions of the foundation.

The grounded front consists of heavy, solid materials rising from the earth in sharp contrast to the more transparent back. The structure moves upward becoming lighter at the downslope side of the house as it opens to the landscape. The main house is a contemporary interpretation of Texas Hill Country post-and-beam construction that exploits regional materials and the expertise of local tradespeople. Without doors, the spaces of the main house flow from one to the other, while the guest room appendage provides a more traditional layout. The materials palette includes concrete, steel, stone, and metals. Texas Hill Country limestone was selected from the site to create the oversized Rumford fireplace central to the living space.

The environmentally mindful design includes a hydronically heated concrete slab on grade. The concrete foundation and walls provide high thermal mass. Large overhangs, covered walkways, and cross ventilation offer protection from the sun and heat. An arbor connects building components functioning as an armature for solar photovoltaic panels that provide power for the property. The landscape consists of drought-tolerant plants native to the area and its ecosystem.

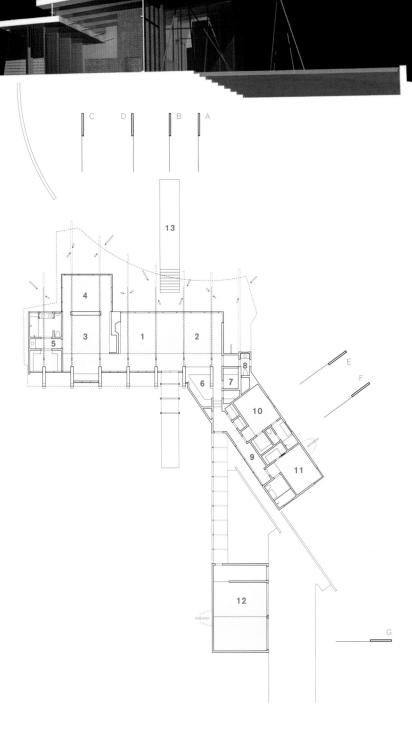

1. LIVING ROOM 2. DINING ROOM 3. LIBRARY 4. MASTER BEDROOM 5. MASTER BATHROOM
6. KITCHEN 7. LAUNDRY 8. POWDER ROOM 9. GALLERY 10. GUEST SUITE A 11. GUEST SUITE B
12. GARAGE 13. POOL

FLOOR PLAN / SECTION

NATURAL

NATURAL

SECTION A

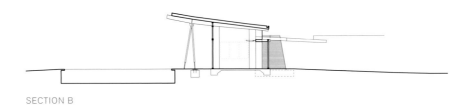

SECTION B

SECTION C

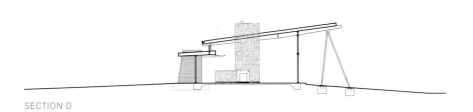

SECTION D

WET

MILWOOD

VENICE, CALIFORNIA

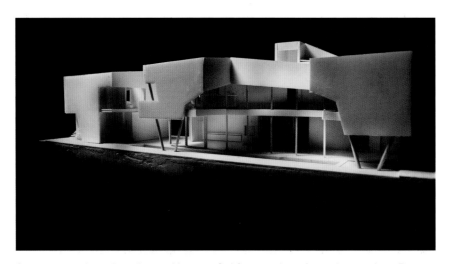

SIMPLE

STATUS: BUILT 2010
SITE: 4,800 SQ.FT.
AREA: 5,000 SQ.FT.
TYPE: RESIDENTIAL
PROGRAM: SINGLE FAMILY
DWELLING
OWNER: ROJAS FAMILY

Set on a tight urban lot in Venice, California, the home is a reflection of its greater site condition. Venice has always been associated with the adjacent Pacific Ocean and canals. The residence itself straddles, weaves, and hovers over the omnipresent body of water.

Apertures in the foundation reveal the subaqueous relationship of the building to the water. A showcase 75-foot-long swimmers' pool is embedded into the foundation and runs the length of the site. Windows are located from the basement facing the pool so swimmers are visible from the interior. Negative space is carved out of the dense building massing, and diffused light penetrates the below grade spaces

from the window. Because the building occupies the majority of the lot, a roof garden reclaims some of the space and is one sustainable feature of the design, along with a 5-kilowatt rooftop solar photovoltaic array, solar heating system for the pool, and energy-efficient construction systems and materials.

The manner in which the water, pool, garden, and house interact blurs the distinction between exterior and interior. Faceted volume surfaces capture reflections, and strategically placed windows frame views to the landscape. This home is an equal blend of nature and the built form, and two opposing elements, but the contrasts become seamless.

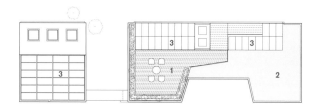

ROOF
1. ROOF DECK 2. ROOF GARDEN 3. SOLAR PANELS

SECOND LEVEL
1. BEDROOM 2. BATHROOM 3. MASTER CLOSET 4. MASTER BEDROOM
5. MASTER BATHROOM 6. STUDIO

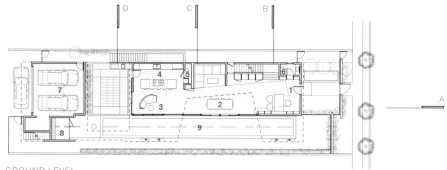

GROUND LEVEL
1. ENTRANCE 2. DINING 3. LIVING 4. KITCHEN 5. DEN 6. POWDER ROOM 7. GARAGE 8. STEAM
ROOM 9. POOL

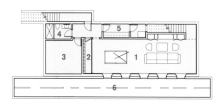

SUBTERRANEAN LEVEL
1. ENTERTAINMENT SPACE 2. WINE CELLAR 3. STORAGE 4. BATHROOM 5. LAUNDRY 6. POOL

SIMPLE

SIMPLE

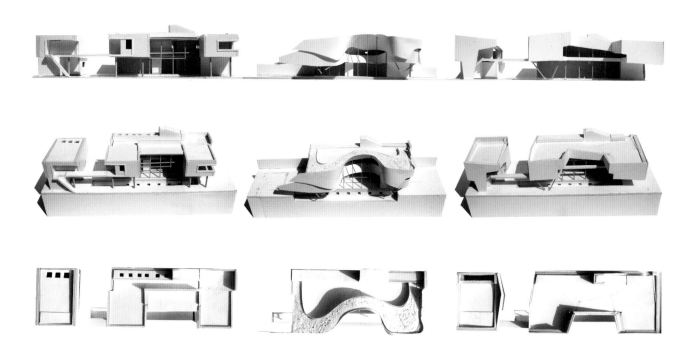

STUDY MODELS

SIMPLE

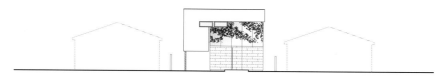

SOUTH ELEVATION

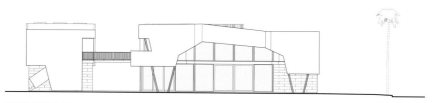

WEST ELEVATION

NORTH ELEVATION

ELEVATIONS

MANUFACTURED

STRUCTURAL SHELL

OP FOLLY

SANTA MONICA,
CALIFORNIA

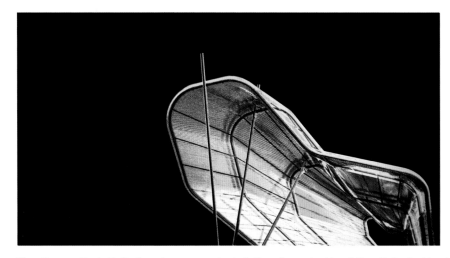

STATUS: BUILT 2007
SITE: 6 ACRES
AREA: 50 SQ.FT.
TYPE: PUBLIC ART
PROGRAM: FOLLY
OWNER: CITY OF SANTA
MONICA

The Ocean Park Folly is a temporary installation for Clover Park in Santa Monica, California. In the spring of 2005, the City of Santa Monica held an open competition to design and build a public installation for the park. The Folly was the winning proposal. It serves as a backdrop for public performances, as well as a place for intimate encounters. The shell's form and materials are inspired by the sea and iconic outdoor arenas, including the Hollywood Bowl and Boston Pops Hatch Shell. Residents and visitors to the seaside community bring multiple interpretations of their own.

The shell is approximately 14 feet long, 12.5 feet wide, and 12 feet high. The surface is a network of woven nylon thread. Layers of transparency suggest a ghost-like enclosure over a steel-frame skeleton. The interplay of light and shadow emphasize the spatial depth of the Folly in the landscape. Ocean breezes pass through the monofilament skin, activating the threads, which in turn cause the shell to resonate with music.

The frame is a kit of parts prefabricated and assembled on site. The base is a series of steel tubes rolled and welded. Computer-generated templates dictated the eccentric shapes of the four steel-pipe arches. The arches affix to the base plate, and each arch is supported with a steel post. The monofilament skin is woven among the steel frames, and over the course of three days, volunteer team members patiently spun the filament network into a mystical blanket of shimmering transparency. Recycled rubber nuggets (grubble) fill the 12.5-foot-diameter ring at the base, and a pillow of recycled rubber is felt underfoot.

SANCTUARY

MAR VISTA

LOS ANGELES,
CALIFORNIA

STATUS: BUILT 2009
SITE: 10,000 SQ.FT.
AREA: 5,200 SQ.FT.
TYPE: RESIDENTIAL
PROGRAM: SINGLE FAMILY
DWELLING
OWNER: GELNER FAMILY

Three discrete building components define this urban villa with a central courtyard garden, a refuge in the middle of Los Angeles that challenges notions of urban versus suburban. The constituent parts lessen the scale of the project and bring the whole into a more intimate relationship with the residents. Despite its location in a large city, the design faces inward, offering privacy and solitude. The living area is contained in the two-story main house. A double-height volume articulates it, where an oversized fireplace extends beyond the roof plane. Folded planes define the roof and walls throughout. Windows perforate the building in a seemingly haphazard manner, but maximize select views and allow light through to the interior.

The pool house and guest wing, a pair of modernist boxes, are restrained counterpoints to the main residence. They mirror each other, bookending the open outdoor space. A swimmers' pool accentuates the axis and appears to float onto a lawn. Meanwhile, the artist's studio rests on pilotis, projecting over the pool, creating enough space for a pool cabana below. Guest quarters are located above the garage and accessed via a bridge that connects the second-story elements and serves as the main entry to the property.

Economical, off-the-shelf materials are used in inventive ways. The assemblage adds depth, texture, and scale to the building massing, from galvanized metal siding with interlocking flat seams, to cement fiberboard used in various proportions as siding, along with exposed steel, glass, and wood. Lower-level glazed walls are open to the courtyard and recessed for sun protection.

ANALOG

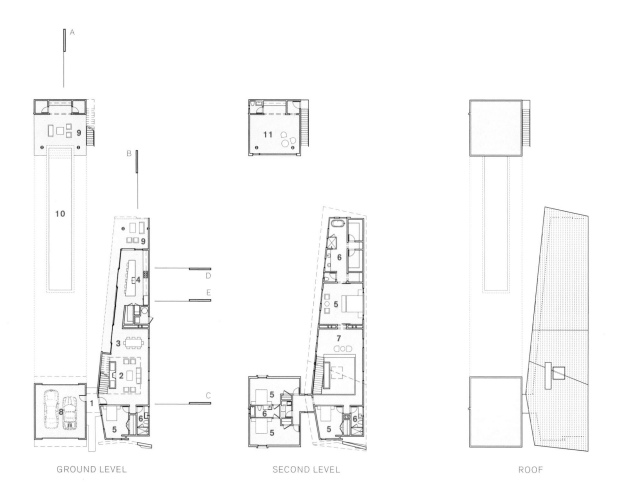

GROUND LEVEL   SECOND LEVEL   ROOF

1. ENTRANCE **2.** LIVING ROOM **3.** DINING ROOM **4.** KITCHEN **5.** BEDROOM **6.** BATHROOM **7.** DEN
8. GARAGE **9.** PATIO **10.** POOL **11.** CABANA

ANALOG

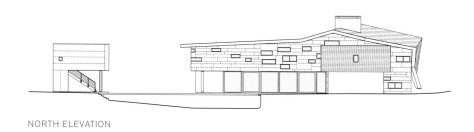

NORTH ELEVATION

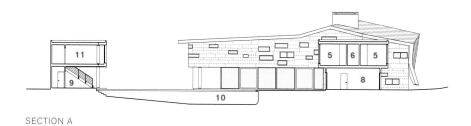

SECTION A

SECTION B

1. ENTRANCE **2.** LIVING ROOM **3.** DINING ROOM **4.** KITCHEN **5.** BEDROOM **6.** BATHROOM **7.** DEN
8. GARAGE **9.** PATIO **10.** POOL **11.** CABANA

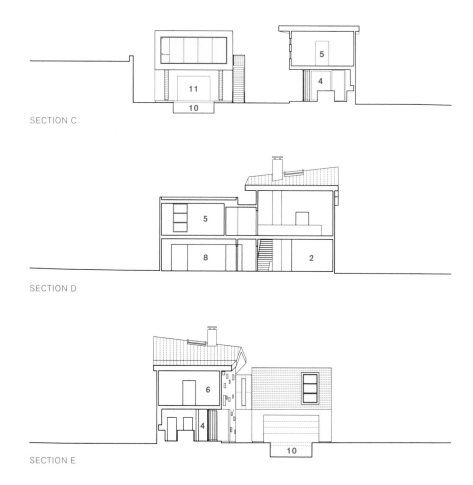

SECTION C

SECTION D

SECTION E

1. ENTRANCE 2. LIVING ROOM 3. DINING ROOM 4. KITCHEN 5. BEDROOM 6. BATHROOM 7. DEN
8. GARAGE 9. PATIO 10. POOL 11. CABANA

ANALOG

SECTIONS

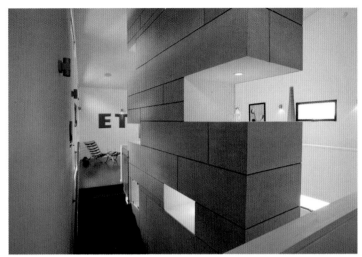

BLACK CAT GARDEN

SUNSET JUNCTION

SILVER LAKE, CALIFORNIA

NATURAL

STATUS: SHORTLISTED 2011
SITE: 3,100 SQ.FT.
AREA: 3,100 SQ.FT.
TYPE: PARK
PROGRAM: LANDSCAPED
PUBLIC SPACE
OWNER: CITY OF
LOS ANGELES

In 2011, Patrick Tighe Architecture was shortlisted for the design of an outdoor public space in the heart of the Silver Lake neighborhood of Los Angeles, at the intersection of two major boulevards. The proposal, the Black Cat Garden at Sunset Junction, serves as a place of remembrance and reflection for the Silver Lake community, celebrating the site and moment where the modern gay civil rights movement began in the U.S. The space pays homage to the Black Cat protesters who, on a February night in 1967 (at the Black Cat Tavern across the street from the site), participated in possibly the largest gay rights demonstration to be held in the U.S. up to that point.

The design uses landscape as an intermediary zone between the pastoral and the urban, the busy and the active, and the chaotic and the serene. A field of folded planes creates an urban mat, applied to the site and extruded, creating a raised plinth. The folding topography is a planar surface of recycled rubber. Circulation paths cut through the garden in a north-south orientation, offering physical and visual connections through lush landscaping, connecting Sunset and Santa Monica Boulevards.

Reinforced concrete planter walls adopt the shape of the section of the folded landscape. Built-in seating is an important design feature of the walls. Lit from underneath, the seats spotlight the decomposed granite paths. Rectangular Corten steel inserts define green slots, containing low-maintenance, drought-tolerant landscaping sprouting from the rubber groundcover. Clustering timber bamboo creates a dense green garden.

From one perspective, an urban forest is evident within the city. Simultaneously, transparency and openness are maintained from the boulevards and along the transverse paths. Thirty-foot-tall columns of light are embedded within the flora, equipped with programmable LEDs, making a rainbow of ever-changing effects possible.

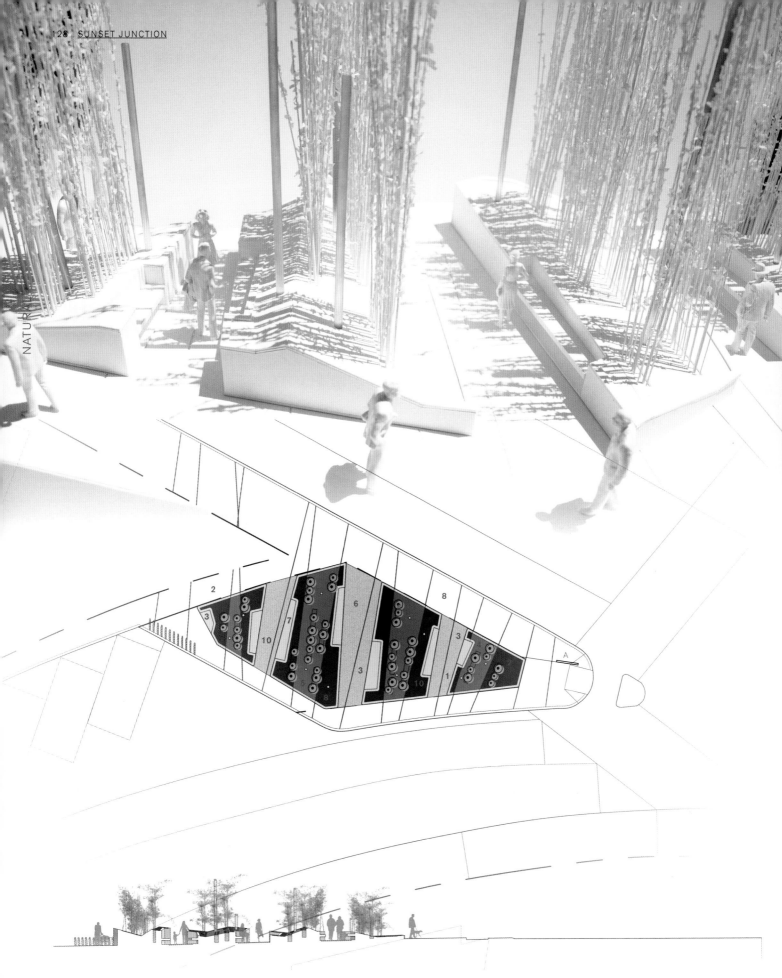

NATURE

1. REINFORCED CONCRETE PLANTER WALLS **2.** RUBBER MAT GROUNDCOVER **3.** OFFICE **4.** CORTEN STEEL PLANTERS **5.** LIGHT COLUMNS **6.** DECOMPOSED GRANITE PATH **7.** TIMBER BAMBOO **8.** EXPANSION JOINTS **9.** BICYCLE RACK **10.** UNDER-MOUNTED LIGHTING

PLAN / SECTION

1.

2.

3.

4.

5.

1. PARK COMPLETE WITH LANDSCAPING 2. PARK WITH BUILT-IN BENCHES AND LIGHT
COLUMNS 3. EXTRUDED SITE WITH CIRCULATION PATHS 4. EXTRUDED SITE 5. URBAN MAT

POINT_COUNTERPOINT

LA LOFT

LOS ANGELES, CALIFORNIA

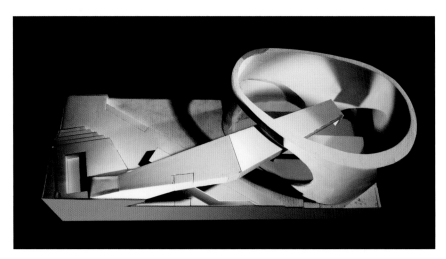

STATUS: BUILT 2006
SITE: 62,000 SQ.FT.
AREA: 1,400 SQ.FT.
TYPE: EXHIBITION SPACE
PROGRAM: LIVE-WORK UNIT
OWNER: LOS ANGELES
MART

SIMPLE

The 1,400-square-foot live-work environment for a creative professional is located in an existing warehouse in downtown Los Angeles. The design consists of distinct entities: the angular, faceted, stone-clad monolith and the free-flowing, organic, elliptical room. A dialogue emerges between them, allowing harmony and conflict to coexist.

Technology is critical to the design in two ways:
To control the environment The inhabitants are able to alter the mood via a central control station. Lighting, music, security, heating, air conditioning, and the display on the media wall are all programmed as part of the user interface. The multifunction media wall serves as an extension of the computer's desktop, a screen for viewing films, and for gaming. It also functions as a virtual art gallery to display our client's photography collection.
To design and fabricate the residence Forms were created via a computer model and fabricated using a

CNC milling process. The raised floor is sheathed with a system of translucent honeycomb panels allowing the LED lighting system below to morph from color to color. Building materials were chosen for their ability to absorb or reflect the changing palette of light.

The elevated flooring transforms into the lounge seating area and the desk of the workstation. In the spa area, stone steps rise to the platform base of the monolith. The raised deck houses an air tub, natural light, and stylized garden. A floating steel fireplace completes the relaxation zone. Undulating walls form a womb-like enclosure, demarcating the kitchen. The skin of the elliptical-shaped room tears away, revealing the bathroom. Walls are pierced with light-sensitive tiles. This is where the overhead cantilevered stone appendage penetrates the embryonic form. The two distinct elements complement, contrast, and violate one another as they coalesce.

SIMPLE

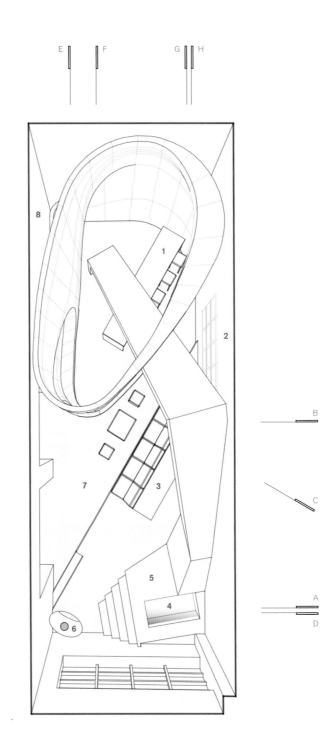

1. KITCHEN 2. MEDIA WALL 3. WORKSTATION 4. SPA 5. RAISED DECK 6. FIREPLACE 7. LIVING ROOM 8. BATHROOM

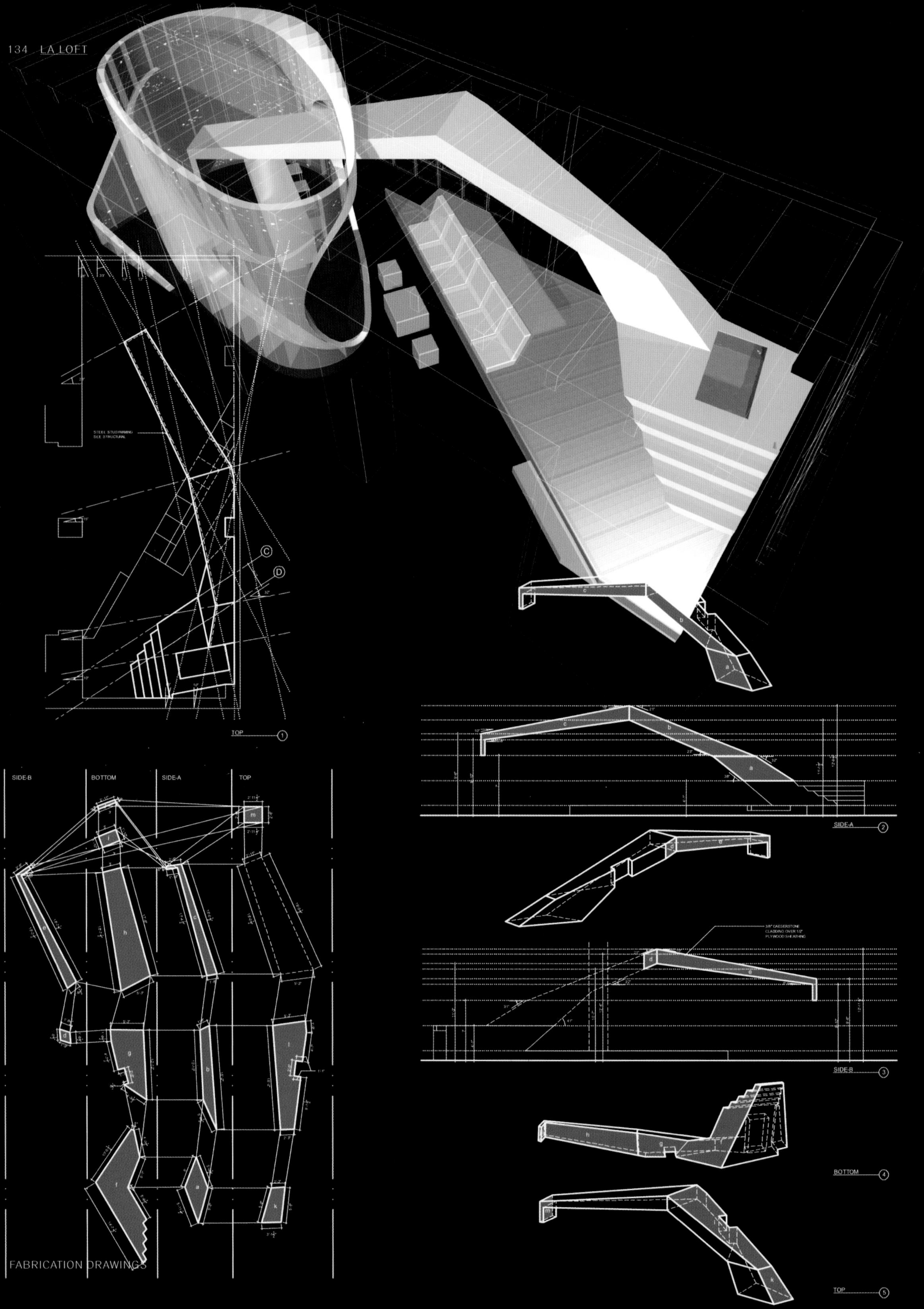

SIMPLE

STEEL STUD FRAMING
SIDE STRUCTURAL

TOP ①

SIDE-B   BOTTOM   SIDE-A   TOP

FABRICATION DRAWINGS

SIDE-A ②

3/8" CAESERSTONE
CLADDING OVER 1/2"
PLYWOOD SHEATHING

SIDE-B ③

BOTTOM ④

TOP ⑤

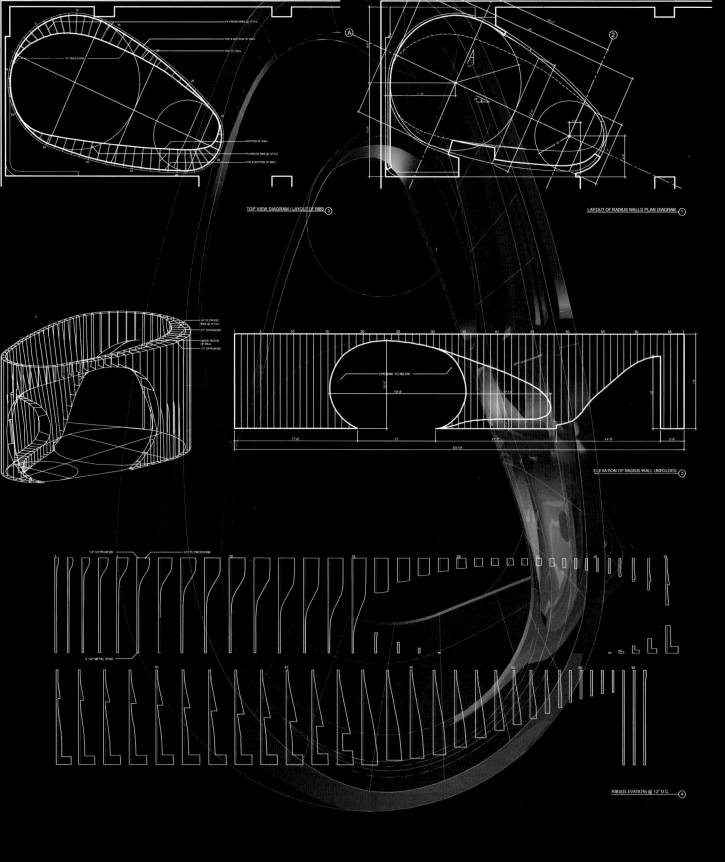

TOP VIEW DIAGRAM / LAYOUT OF RIBS ②

LAYOUT OF RADIUS WALLS PLAN DIAGRAM ①

ELEVATION OF RADIUS WALL UNFOLDED ③

OPENING TO BELOW

RIBS(ELEVATION) @ 12" O.C. ④

FABRICATION DRAWINGS

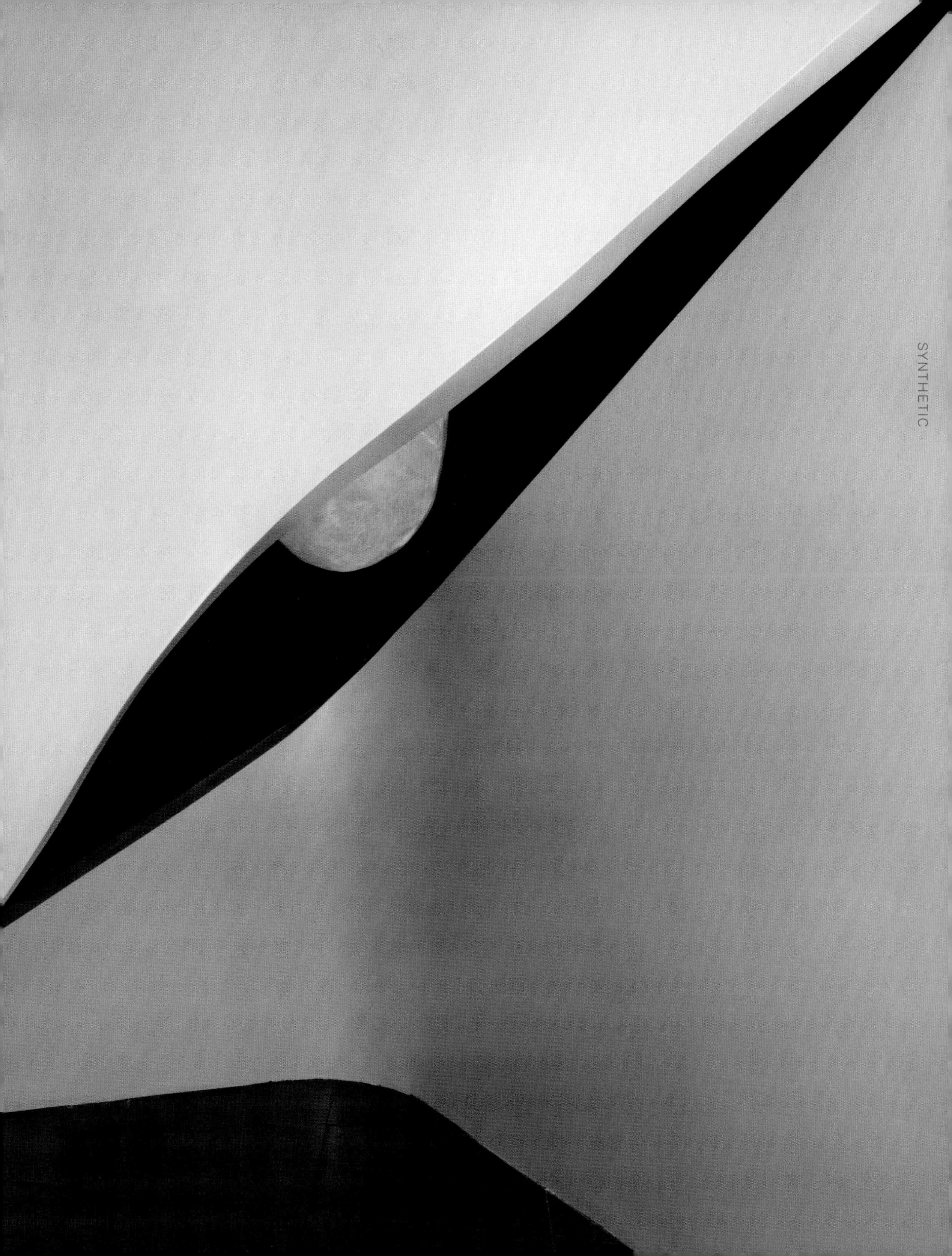

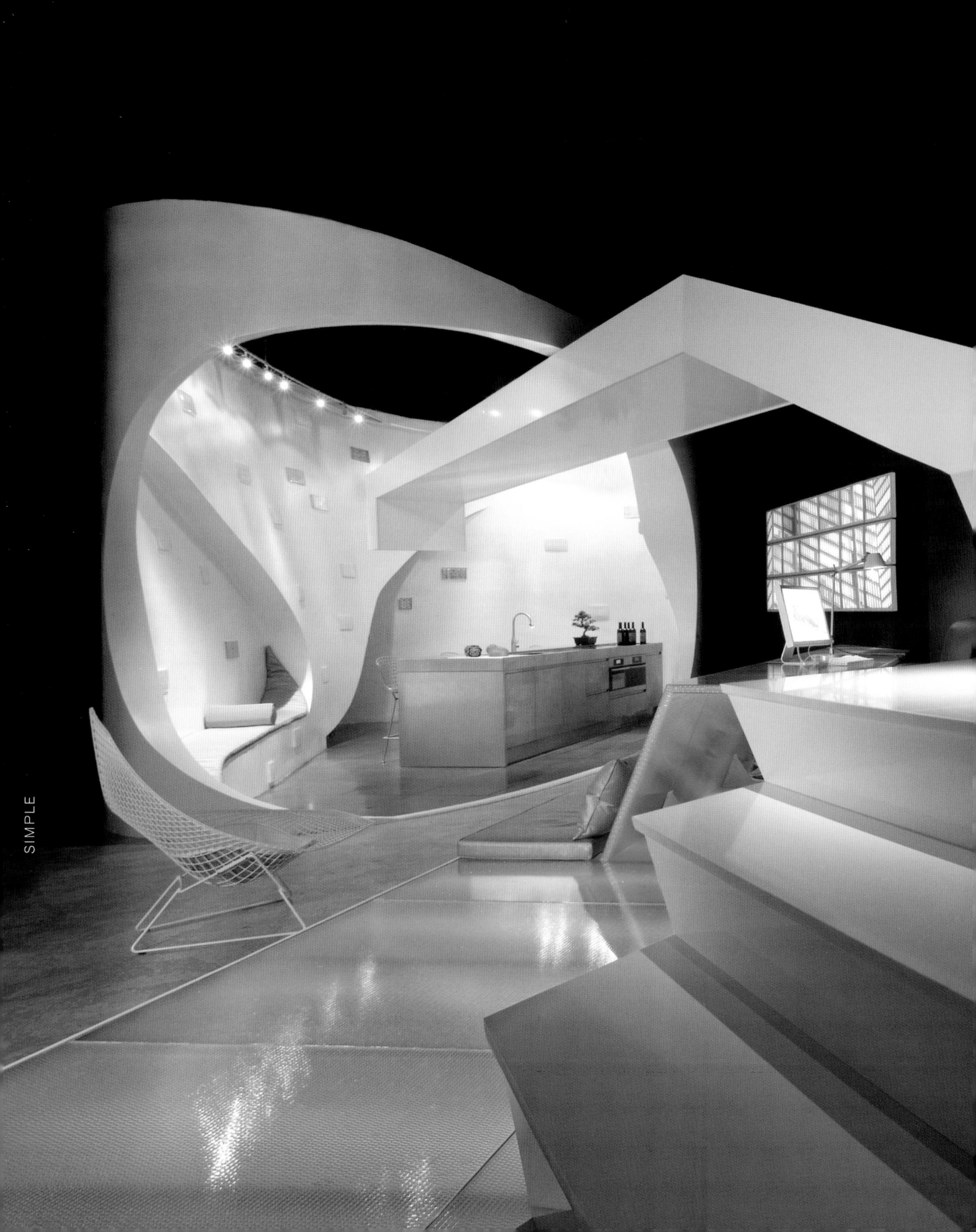

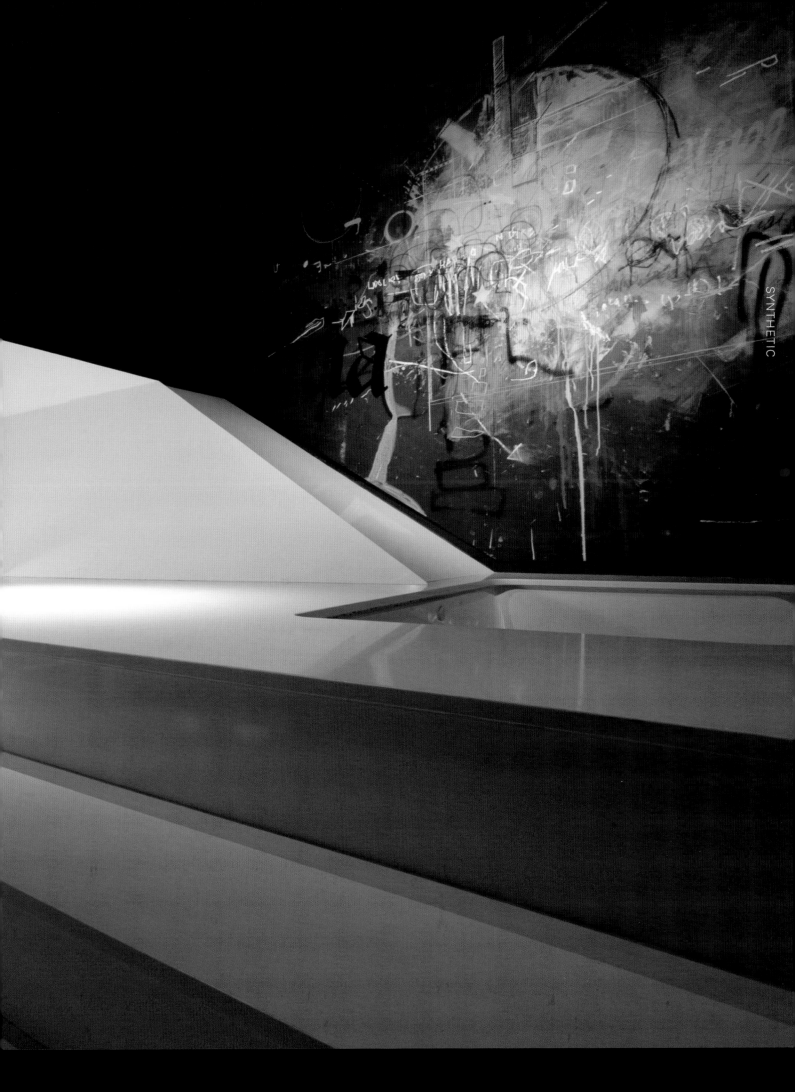

PLUG AND PLAY

NODUL(AR) HOUSE

LOS ANGELES, CALIFORNIA

STATUS: IN DEVELOPMENT
SITE: VARIES
AREA: 30 TO 3,200 SQ.FT.
TYPE: RESIDENTIAL
PROGRAM: SINGLE FAMILY
DWELLING
OWNER: JERICHO HOMES

The design for Nodul(ar) house integrates new processes and manufacturing technologies with two long-established concepts—prefabrication and the modular. Nodul(ar) house translates the modular into "nodal" form driven by parameters of performance and technology. The hybrid residence makes use of a series of prefabricated utility nodes. These nodes attach to a prefabricated home system that utilizes high performance aluminum extrusions with various infill panels.

The homes are rectilinear in shape, and a series of self-contained utility pieces, primarily circular in form, are available and include configurations of bathrooms, kitchens, and stair towers. The pieces are fully realized in a factory and affixed to the foundations on site. The system is a series of shared parts. A central connector spine contains utilities that include plumbing, electrical, and venting. Attached is an inner liner molded to the function of the node and protected by an outer cylindrical shell. Insulation is sandwiched between the two layers.

The nodes share common footprints and the units are stackable, allowing for flexibility and customization. The pieces are in development and will be fabricated using environmentally responsible fiberglass with the necessary protective coatings. The design of the Nodul(ar) house exploits the benefits of variability and adaptability made possible by well-harnessed technological systems, while at the same time maintaining the efficiency and economics that result from uniformity.

MANUFACTURED

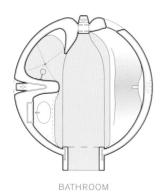

BATHROOM

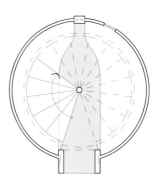

KITCHEN

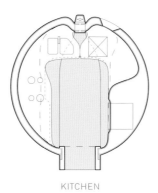

STAIR TOWER

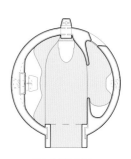

POWDER ROOM

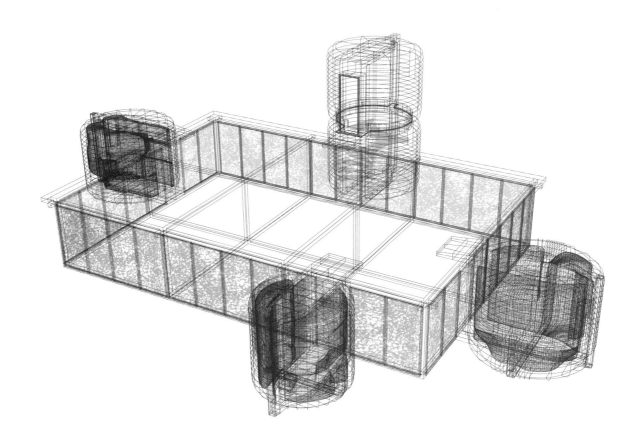

FLOOR PLANS / PERSPECTIVE

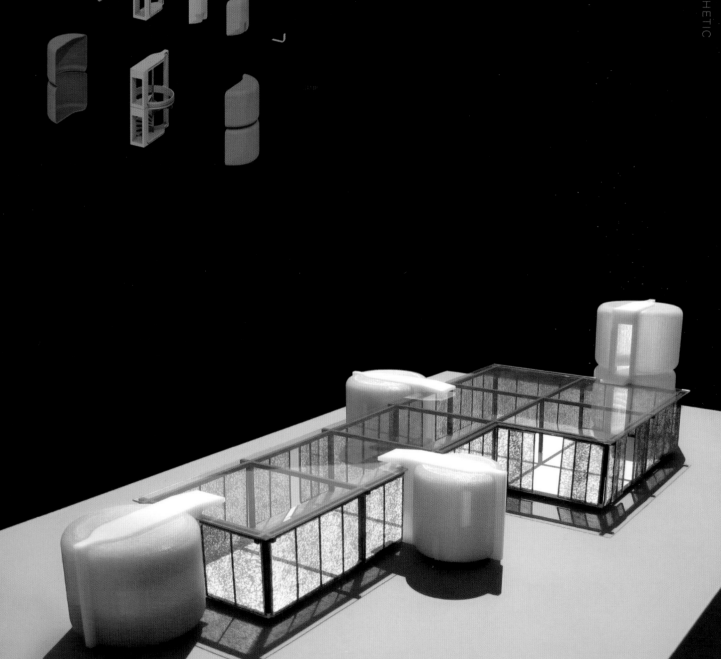

IN LIVING COLOR

MOVING PICTURE COMPANY

SANTA MONICA,
CALIFORNIA

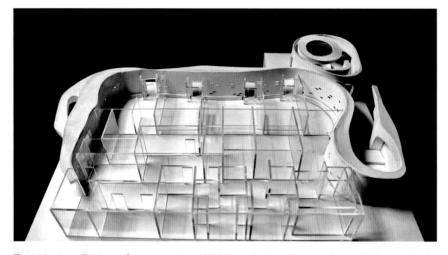

STATUS: BUILT 2011
SITE: 48,000 SQ.FT.
AREA: 8,200 SQ.FT.
TYPE: OFFICE
ENVIRONMENT
PROGRAM: POST
PRODUCTION, EDIT BAYS,
OFFICES, MEETING AREAS
OWNER: TECHNICOLOR

The Moving Picture Company is a UK-based visual effects post-production company—a forerunner in the visual effects and animation fields for the feature film, advertising, music, and television industries. The 8,200-square-foot facility is located in a generic office building in downtown Santa Monica, California, which serves as their U.S. headquarters. The facility includes grading rooms, editing bays, conference rooms, open and closed offices, client areas, production spaces, entertaining areas, tape vault, mechanical rooms, machine rooms, exterior terraces, and support spaces. Given the company is highly regarded for its work in the field of color manipulation in film, the project focuses on light as it relates to color. Forms and patterns are produced using light studies in which light is analyzed and modeled three-dimensionally. Frames from animation are chosen and layered to organize spatial qualities and movement throughout the office environment. An organic, sinuous spine weaves its way through the suite. An attached soffit grows from the serpentine walls functioning as an armature for cable trays and mechanical and electrical systems. Light portals pierce the organic forms and are equipped with programmable LED lighting. Patterns derived from the animated light studies are projected onto the laser-cut walls and circumscribe the interior.

Motion is expressed throughout the space reinforced by the lighting scheme. Groups of LED lights penetrate the serpentine wall and emit color. The aluminum pieces are custom-fabricated to house the LED fixtures. They are flush with the outside, public face of the wall and protrude into the private rooms, adding texture and creating a more intimate scale in the larger context. The lighting is programmable, offering various intensities and color options, subject to our client's desire.

ACTUAL

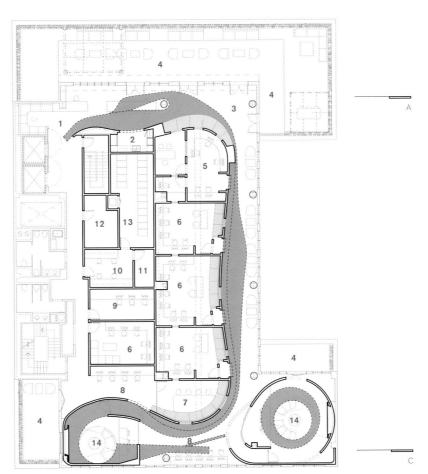

1. LOBBY 2. KITCHEN 3. COMMON AREA 4. TERRACE 5. OFFICE 6. PROJECT ROOM
7. CONFERENCE ROOM 8. OPEN OFFICE 9. EDIT ROOM 10. TAPE OP ROOM 11. SCAN
12. FILM / TAPE VAULT 13. MACHINE ROOM 14. GRADING ROOM

ACTUAL

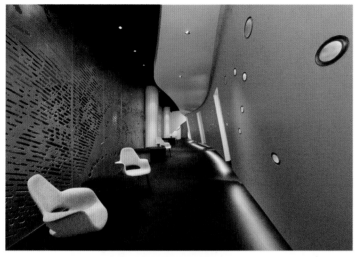

ACTUAL

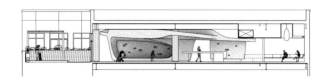

SECTION A

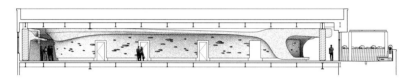

SECTION B

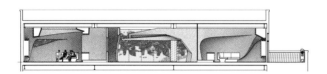

SECTION C

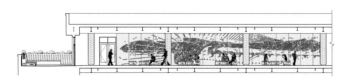

SECTION D

SECTIONS

ACTUAL

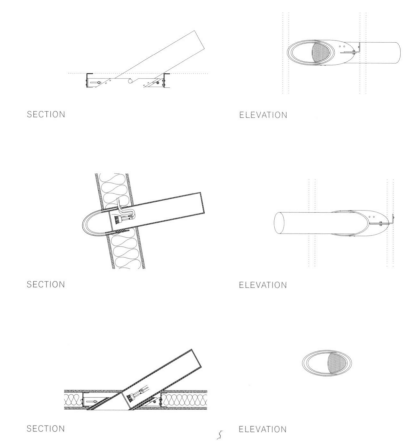

SECTION   ELEVATION

SECTION   ELEVATION

SECTION   ELEVATION

EMBEDDED CUSTOM LIGHT FIXTURE

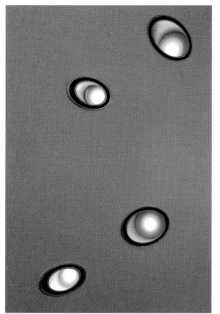

CELTIC KNOT

WEST CORK ARTS CENTER

SKIBBEREEN, CO CORK,
IRELAND

ACTUAL

STATUS: COMPETITION
SITE: 16,000 SQ.FT.
AREA: 6,500 SQ.FT.
TYPE: ARTS CENTER
PROGRAM: EXHIBITION,
CLASSROOMS, LECTURE
HALLS, CAFÉ, PUBLIC
SPACES
OWNER: WEST CORK ARTS
CENTER

Celtic symbolism, literary references, Irish folklore, and native traditions are interpreted spatially to create a dynamic 21st-century arts center in West Cork, Ireland. The past, present, and future of a culturally and intellectually rich region inform building design: a proud history, present-day zeitgeist, and promising future. The project also integrates the traditional art forms of the area. Conceived as a field of interconnected strands of activity, the building components intertwine, creating a unified whole.

The project is a networked system of connectivity. Pedestrian traffic flow, view orientations, and sensitivity to scale combine to create its form. The dense scheme encloses a central outdoor courtyard. The shimmering building skin is lit from within. Metaphorically, the center serves as a beacon for the arts within the town center. The project has an open plan and wraps a central exterior courtyard.

A double-height atrium space serves as the entrance foyer and flows into the gallery and performance hall, all located at the ground level. The artists' studios with an adjacent outdoor courtyard are a half level below grade. Retail space is located at the entrance to the site.

Site conditions are carefully considered. Along Caol Stream, the structure is low and unassuming, rising toward the back of the site. Strategically placed, it accommodates views from the shopping streets. A gesture is made towards Main Street, where the building opens to the north and greets visitors. The façade is transparent at the northern exposure, as glass walls ring the courtyard. Northern light filters through the clerestory window above, washing the gallery and circulation spaces. The gallery protrudes to the north over the stream.

ACTUAL

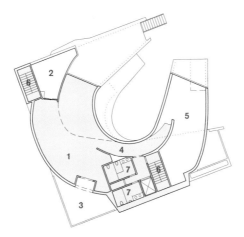

THIRID LEVEL
1. GALLERY 2. ADMINISTRATION 3. TERRACE 4. CIRCULATION 5. OPEN TO BELOW 6. STAIR
CORE 7. TOILET ROOM

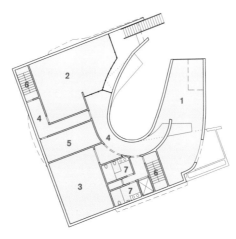

SECOND LEVEL
1. GALLERY 2. DANCE STUDIO 3. WORKSPACE 4. CIRCULATION 5. CHANGING ROOM 6. STAIR
CORE 7. TOILET ROOM

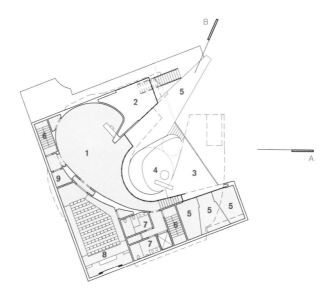

GROUND LEVEL
1. GALLERY 2. COMMERCIAL SPACE 3. ARTISTS' COURT 4. COURTYARD 5. ARTIST'S STUDIO
6. STAIR CORE 7. TOILET ROOM 8. PERFORMANCE SPACE 9. STORAGE

ACTUAL

NORTH ELEVATION

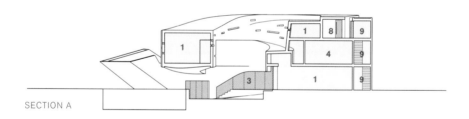

EAST ELEVATION

SECTION A

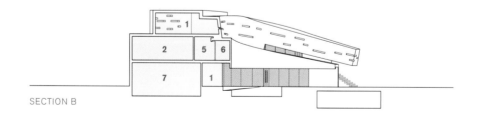

SECTION B

1. GALLERY 2. WORKSPACE 3. COURTYARD 4. DANCE STUDIO 5. TOILET ROOM 6. CIRCULATION
7. PERFORMANCE SPACE 8. ADMINISTRATION 9. STAIR CORE

ELEVATIONS / SECTIONS

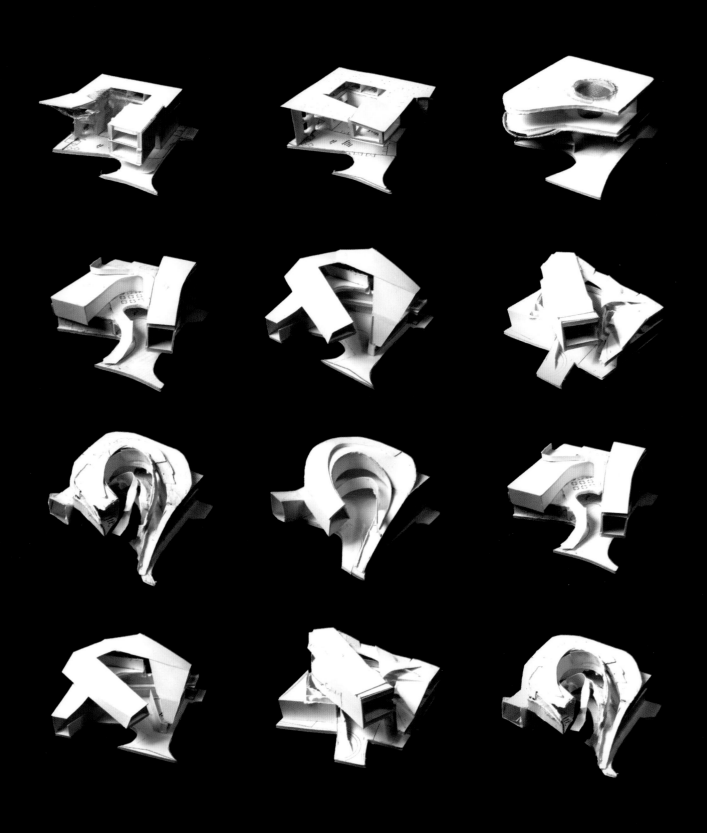

ACTUAL

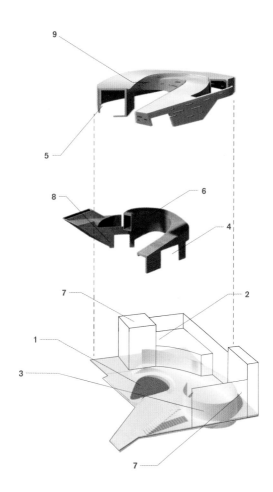

1. COURTYARD 2. PERFORMANCE SPACE 3. THERMAL MASS WALL 4. GALLERY A 5. GALLERY B
6. ADMINISTRATION 7. CIRCULATION CORE 8. ARTIST STUDIOS 9. DANCE STUDIO

BUILDING COMPONENTS

DENSE CITY IS GOOD

SIERRA BONITA MIXED-USE AFFORDABLE HOUSING

WEST HOLLYWOOD,
CALIFORNIA

SIMPLE

STATUS: BUILT 2012
SITE: 13,000 SQ.FT.
AREA: 70,000 SQ.FT.
TYPE: MIXED USE
PROGRAM: 42 APARTMENTS,
COMMERCIAL SPACE
OWNER: WEST HOLLYWOOD
COMMUNITY HOUSING
CORP

The mixed-use affordable housing in West Hollywood addresses a severe housing shortage for residents living with disabilities. The 70,000-square-foot program responds to the city's mandate to maximize units on site to increase density in the city's urban core. On a 13,000-square-foot lot in a dense urban corridor, the building contains 42 one-bedroom units arranged around a central courtyard, near commercial and retail spaces, located along Santa Monica Boulevard. Parking is provided at the subterranean levels and at grade.

Each apartment has a private front porch overlooking the courtyard garden, facilitating social interaction among the residents and offering a respite from the boulevard. Additional communal spaces are provided for the residents and for public use. A steel brace frame carves out the interior void for the courtyard to satisfy requirements for outdoor space allotment. The design of the eccentric brace frame core is essential to the project and seen as a five-story lattice in the

courtyard. The geometry of the frame is used as a pattern for the north and south façades of the building. The structure demonstrates one of the city's values of environmental responsibility and its commitment to green building and sustainable design, serving as a pilot project for the Green Building Ordinance, as well.

Passive solar design strategies include: a north-south orientation for the units, positioning the building to control solar cooling loads, orienting the building for exposure to prevailing winds, designing windows to maximize daylight, minimizing west-facing glazing, and designing units to maximize natural ventilation.

Photovoltaic panels integrated into the façade and roof supply most of the peak-load electricity demand, while serving as a trellis for shading the rooftop decks. A solar hydronic system provides residents with free hot water. The bamboo forest in the inner courtyard creates a cooling microclimate.

SIMPLE

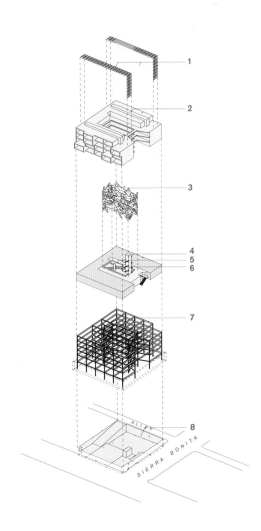

1. PHOTOVOLTAIC CANOPY 2. RESIDENTIAL UNITS 3. BRACED-FRAME CORE 4. COMMERCIAL / RETAIL 5. COURTYARD GARDEN 6. CIRCULATION / RESIDENTIAL 7. STEEL FRAME STRUCTURE 8. SUBTERRANEAN PARKING LEVEL

BUILDING COMPONENTS

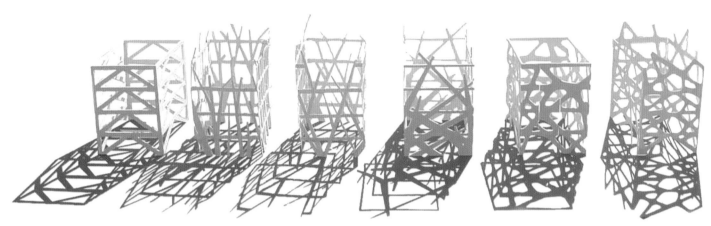

DERIVATIONS OF THE BRACED-FRAME CORE

SIMPLE

ECCENTRIC BRACED-FRAME / STRUCTURE TO LATTICE

ECCENTRIC BRACED-FRAME

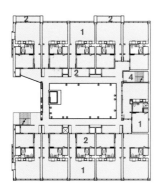

FOURTH LEVEL

FIFTH LEVEL

SECOND LEVEL

THIRD LEVEL

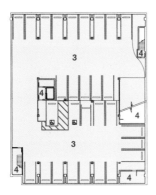

SUBTERRANEAN LEVEL

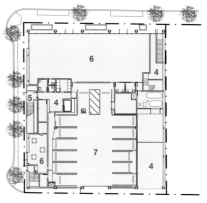

GROUND LEVEL

SIMPLE

1. RESIDENTIAL **2.** PRIVATE OPEN SPACE **3.** RESIDENTIAL PARKING **4.** CIRCULATION / UTILITY
5. COMMON OPEN SPACE **6.** RETAIL / OFFICE / COMMUNITY ROOM **7.** COMMERCIAL PARKING

FLOOR PLANS

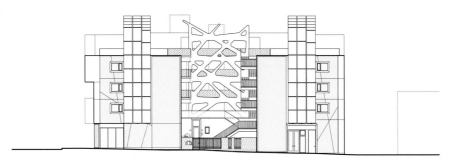

WEST ELEVATION

NORTH ELEVATION

SIMPLE

Q   R   S   T   U

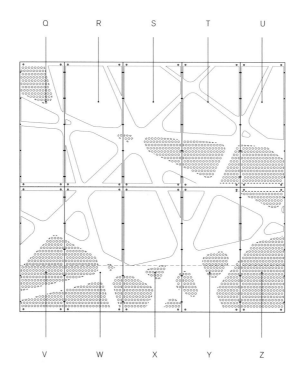

V   W   X   Y   Z

SIMPLE

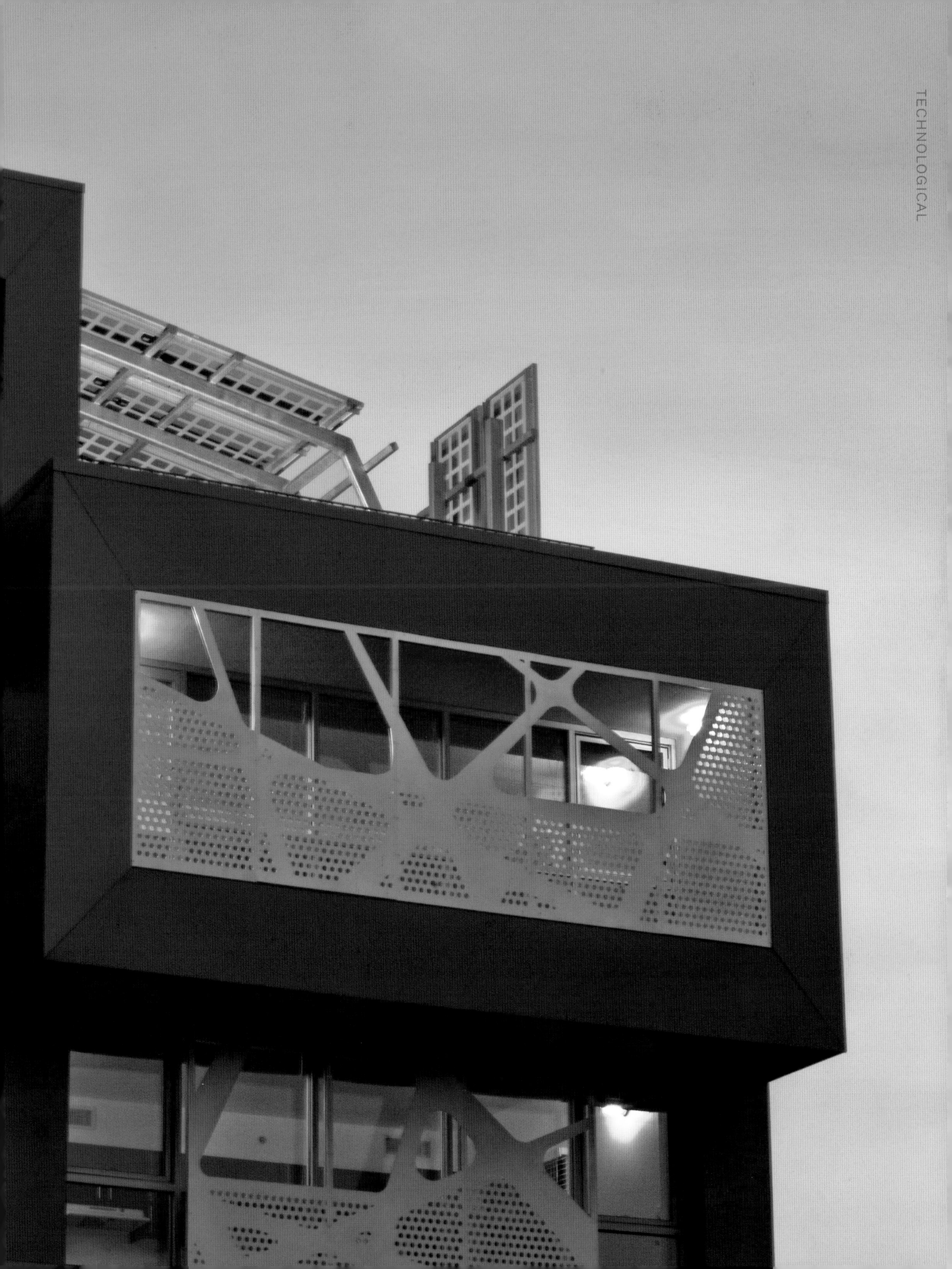

MANUFACTURED

FOAM REDUX

SPRAY ON HOUSE

JOSHUA TREE, CALIFORNIA

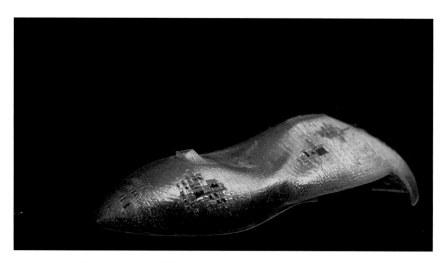

STATUS: IN DEVELOPMENT
SITE: 5 ACRES
AREA: 2,700 SQ.FT.
TYPE: RESIDENTIAL
PROGRAM: SINGLE FAMILY
DWELLING
OWNER: ARNAUD
GREGORIO

Spray On House is a 2,700-square-foot, self-sustaining desert retreat on a remote site adjacent to Joshua Tree National Park, California. Research for the project explored the potential of renewable polyurethane spray foam as a building material—in particular, advances in spray foam technology and the latent possibilities of a material that, until recently, has been used primarily for insulation. We uncovered characteristics that include limitless formal attributes, reduced environmental impact, ease of construction, and competitive pricing.

The typology advances a new structural materiality that allows for fluid form-making with structural strength in a single substance. Advances in the environmental qualities associated with spray foams, such as new soy-based products, make the material and technology not only a viable option but also a cost-effective and innovative solution compared to traditional construction methods. Spray On House is an extremely adaptable method of construction. The foam yields high structural strength and given

its nearly instant cure-time, can conform to almost any shape, making it ideal for a broad range of programmatic and site conditions. It is both the interior and exterior of the structure, allowing for fully integrated environments.

Power is provided via a 5-kilowatt solar photovoltaic system. Other environmentally friendly amenities include a water collection device, water storage tank, generator, and compost toilets. The home uses 5-pounds-per-cubic-foot density foam with steel reinforcement. The rebar cage is embedded within the layers of spray foam and grounded to the site via a continuous spread footing. The materials and the building form provide a high thermal mass, advantageous in the arid climate. An additional exterior fluid coating will be applied over the foam for fire resistance and UV exposure. The single source building system addresses the challenges of transporting large quantities of building materials and numerous subcontractors to the remote desert site, further reducing costs and environmental impact.

MANUFACTURED

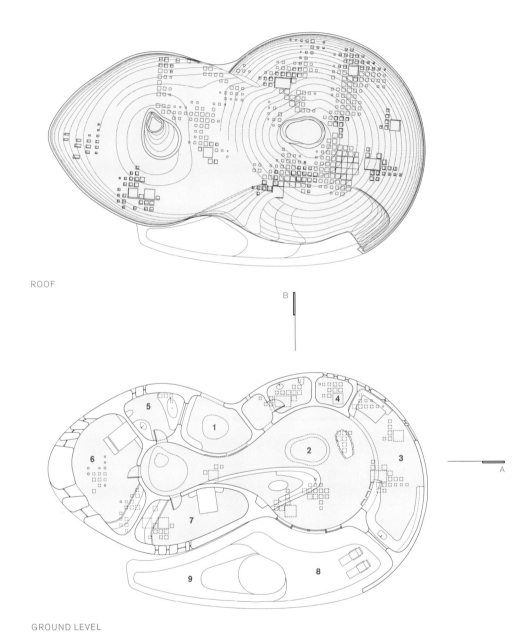

ROOF

B

A

GROUND LEVEL

1. ENTRANCE 2. LIVING ROOM 3. KITCHEN 4. MECHANICAL 5. BATHROOM 6. MASTER BEDROOM
7. BEDROOM 8. DECK 9. POOL

FLOOR PLAN

MANUFACTURED

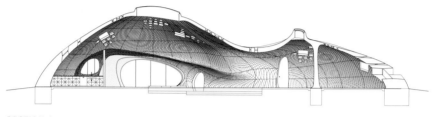

SECTION A

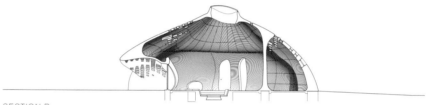

SECTION B

ELEVATION

COMPULSORY FIGURE

SOCHI OLYMPIC PAVILION

SOCHI, RUSSIA

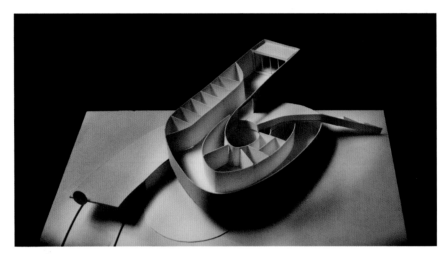

STATUS: SHORTLISTED 2013
SITE: 20,000 SQ.FT.
AREA: 15,000 SQ.FT.
TYPE: EXHIBITION HALL
PROGRAM: GALLERIES,
THEATER MEETINGS,
RECEPTION AREA
OWNER: RUSSIAN RAILWAYS

The Olympic Pavilion was designed for the 2014 Olympic Games in Sochi, Russia. The project, commissioned by Russian Railways, draws upon the strength of the railway and uses movement to express the architectural form. The building is designed to spiral around a central exterior space consisting of a fountain and a frozen plaza for ice skating. The ramped spiral culminates in a multifunctional common area used primarily for receptions. The dominant spiral form of the building has a dynamism and energy, and its sense of movement is evocative of the compulsory figures a skater performs.

The interior circulation spine serves two significant functions: it is the framework to which all programmatic elements are linked and also doubles as the continuous exhibition space. The exterior building cladding is a semi-transparent gradient of openings. The perforations in the building skin pay homage to Russian folkloric patterning, including handmade lace and embroidered fabrics.

Programmatically, in addition to its principal function as an exhibition hall, the 15,000-square-foot building accommodates the following: reception areas, ticketing, cafés, private offices, restrooms, and service areas. A grand hall frames a spectacular view of the mountainous surroundings and opens onto an exterior terrace that overlooked the Olympic Village. A grand exterior stair led visitors back to the winter wonderland of the 2014 Winter Olympics.

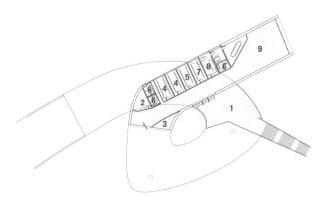

TOP LEVEL
1. BALCONY   2. STORAGE   3. PHOTO STUDIO   4. RZD TV STUDIO   5. MARKETING / PRESS SERVICES
6. BATHROOMS   7. TECHNICAL SPECIALISTS   8. RECEIVING OFFICE   9. HALL FOR PARTIES

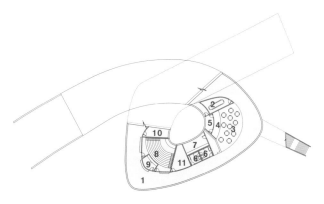

MID LEVEL
1. EXHIBITION SPACE   2. VIP LOUNGE   3. RESTAURANT   4. STAGE FOR ARTISTS   5. MAKE-UP ROOM
6. BATHROOM   7. KITCHEN   8. CINEMA   9. PROJECTION ROOM   10. PHOTO STUDIO   11. STORAGE

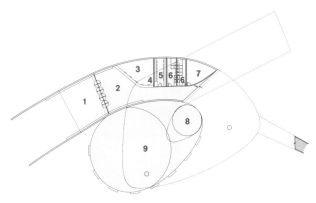

GROUND LEVEL
1. ENTRANCE   2. LOUNGE ZONE   3. RECEPTION   4. RAILWAY TICKETING OFFICE   5. DUTY OFFICER/
SECURITY   6. BATHROOM   7. STORAGE   8. WATER FALL   9. SKATING RINK

ACTUAL

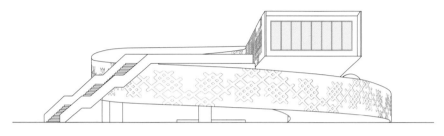

NORTH ELEVATION

ACTUAL

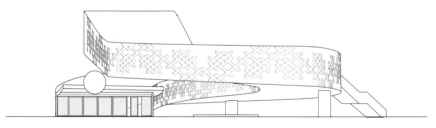

SOUTH ELEVATION

ELEVATIONS

VOIDED MASS DTLA

GRAND AVENUE

LOS ANGELES, CALIFORNIA

ACTUAL

STATUS: SHORTLISTED 2011
SITE: 2 ACRES
AREA: 275,000 SQ.FT.
TYPE: MIXED USE
PROGRAM: APARTMENTS,
RETAIL, EXHIBITION SPACE,
RESTAURANTS
OWNER: THE RELATED
COMPANY

In 2011, this project for a mixed-use building on Grand Avenue in downtown Los Angeles was shortlisted to be the first of the Grand Avenue Development projects, serving as a catalyst for future initiatives. The 20-story structure consists of 250 residential units, with retail and commercial space located at the street level and three levels of parking provided below Grand. Shared common amenities and support programs for the residents exist at the plinth located at the second level.

The building serves as a backdrop to the iconic Disney Concert Hall and the adjacent Broad Museum. The commercial components of the building open up to a plaza at street level. The building sets back at grade in both plan and section, defining an outdoor space for public use. The urban plaza establishes a connection to the adjacent Broad Museum, the nearby Disney Concert Hall, the Dorothy Chandler Pavilion, Museum of Contemporary Art, and the rest of downtown.

Conceived as a white volume with varying amounts of transparency and reflectivity, the building envelope subtly activates the simple massing. A series of slits penetrates the massing of the building, breaking down the scale and offering relief within the fenestration. Each void is programmed for a specific use. For example, one void allows light and air to enter the building, another is for circulation through the building, and a third is used to carve out a strong connection (in section) from Hope Street up to Grand.

ACTUAL

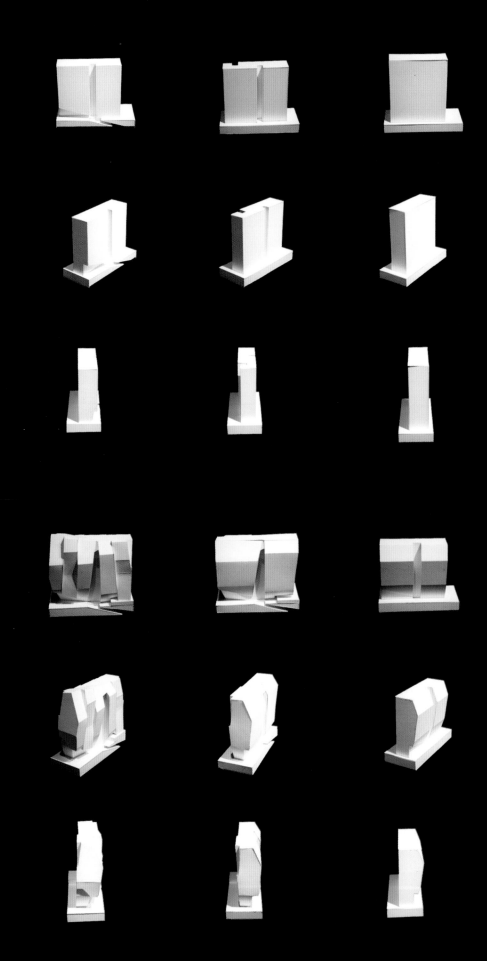

THIRD LEVEL   20TH LEVEL   21ST LEVEL

1. ELEVATOR **2.** LOBBY **3.** TWO-BEDROOM APARTMENT **4.** ONE-BEDROOM APARTMENT **5.** STUDIO APARTMENT **6.** BALLROOM

ACTUAL

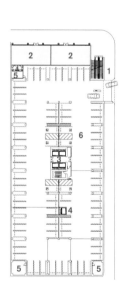

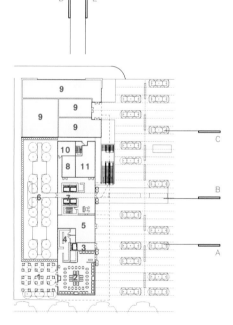

PARKING LEVEL
1. ENTRANCE TO GROUND LEVEL
2. COMMERCIAL SPACE **3.** ELEVATORS
4. RESTAURANT ELEVATOR **5.** STORAGE
6. PARKING

PLAZA LEVEL
1. OUTDOOR DINING **2.** RESTAURANT
3. RESTAURANT ELEVATOR **4.** KITCHEN
5. RETAIL **6.** GARDEN **7.** ELEVATORS
8. MAIL ROOM **9.** COMMERCIAL / RETAIL
10. STORAGE **11.** LEASING OFFICE

SECOND LEVEL
1. TWO-BEDROOM APARTMENT
2. STUDIO APARTMENT
3. ONE-BEDROOM APARTMENT
4. ELEVATORS **5.** LOBBY
6. SCREENING ROOM **7.** FITNESS
8. TECHNOLOGY ROOM **9.** STORAGE
10. CABANA **11.** POOL **12.** JACUZZI

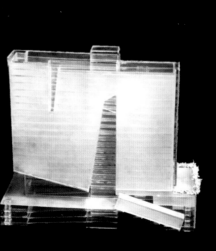

ACTUAL

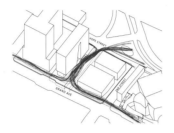

PEDESTRIAN CIRCULATION

VEHICULAR ACCESS

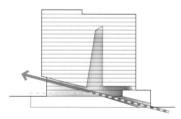

PEDESTRIAN CIRCULATION

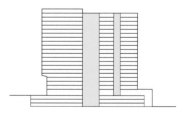

VERTICAL CIRCULATION

MANUFACTURED

NESTED

TAICHUNG FINE ARTS MUSEUM AND LIBRARY

TAICHUNG, TAIWAN

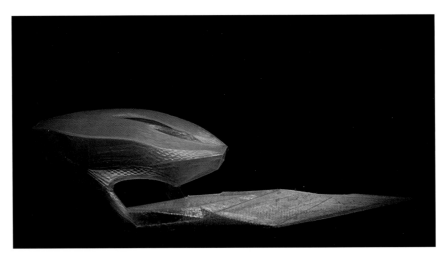

STATUS: COMPETITION 2012
SITE: 16 ACRES
AREA: 120,000 SQ.FT.
TYPE: CULTURAL CENTER
PROGRAM: MUSEUM,
LIBRARY, PUBLIC PARKS
OWNER: CITY OF TAICHUNG

The Taichung City Cultural Center is sited at the entrance to Taichung Gateway Park. It will provide citizens with a multipurpose cultural, artistic, and recreational facility, including a world-class museum of fine arts and public library—a symbol of progress, not only for the city but also for Taiwan. It will command an international presence, promoting new art forms, in addition to valuable resources for local residents. The technologically advanced, environmentally conscious scheme projects a progressive vision.

The landscape rises to meet the building at the terminus of the major axis. A grand exhibition hall spans the length of the building along the north-south axis. The facility is designed for optimum flexibility, capable of housing a variety of venues. The large exterior mall functions as a public gathering space. The honorific grand stair and mall's landscape provide a civic presence for the building within the park.

From inside the grand hall, there are framed views to the landscape beyond, forming a strong connection between nature and the built form. The building is open and transparent at the street and burrowed into the landscape at the south. The library is an open plan for versatility, future growth, and accommodation of various new multimedia technologies.

Several "buildings within the building" are articulated as special programmatic elements including the children's reading room, the technology room, and the exhibition hall. The library and museum are designed to bring the exterior in and through the building. The pattern derived from the landscape reflects onto the building surfaces, becoming a means by which the interior surfaces are also penetrated.

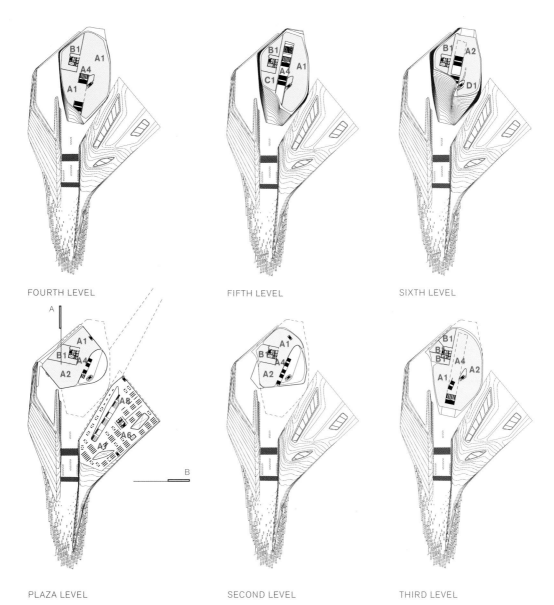

FOURTH LEVEL

FIFTH LEVEL

SIXTH LEVEL

PLAZA LEVEL

SECOND LEVEL

THIRD LEVEL

A1. PERMANENT EXHIBITION AREA **A2.** SPECIAL EXHIBITION AREA **A3.** SMALL THEATER **A4.** LOUNGE
A5. LITERATURE READING AREA **A6.** ART READING AREA **A7.** FOREIGN LANGUAGE **B1.** ARCHIVE
C1. CORPORATE ART EXCHANGE AREA **D1.** LIBRARY

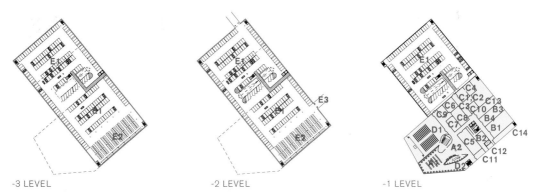

-3 LEVEL

-2 LEVEL

-1 LEVEL

A1. MULTIMEDIA & INTERNET RESOURCES **A2.** YOUNG ADULTS READING AREA **B1.** EDITING OFFICE
B2. MULTIMEDIA OPERATIONS **B3.** COMPUTER INFORMATION CENTER **B4.** CIRCULATION OFFICE
C1. DIRECTOR OFFICE **C2.** DEPUTY DIRECTOR OFFICE **C3.** SECRETARY DESK **C4.** ETHICS OFFICE
C5. SECRETARY **C6.** ACCOUNTING ROOM **C7.** HR ROOM **C8.** PROMOTION SECTION **C9.** CONSULTATION
SERVICE **C10.** ADMIN. MEETING ROOM **C11.** MAIL COUNTER **C12.** CENTRAL CONTROL ROOM **C13.** CENTRAL
ADMIN. STORAGE **C14.** VOLUNTEER OFFICE **D1.** CONFERENCE HALL **D2.** E-LEARNING CLASSROOMS
E1. CAR PARKING **E2.** SCOOTER PARKING **E3.** DRIVEWAY TO CONVENTION CENTER

MANUFACTURED

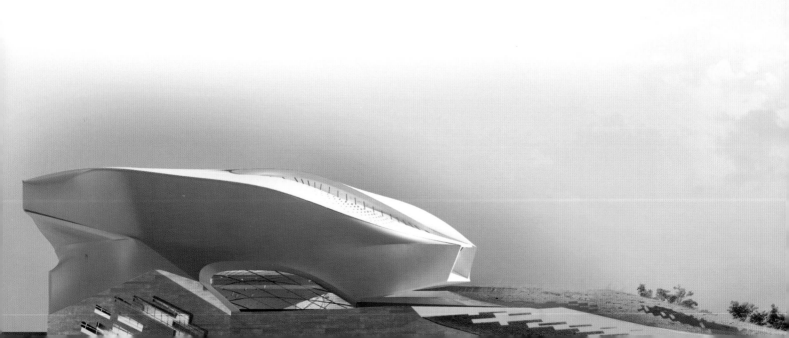

WHITE NOISE

OUT OF MEMORY

LOS ANGELES, CALIFORNIA

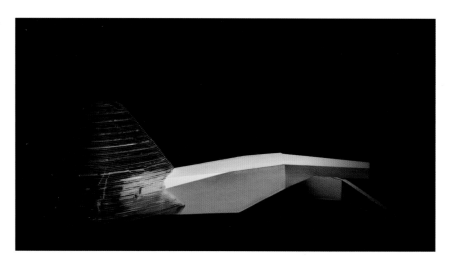

ACTUAL

STATUS: BUILT 2012
SITE: 1,500 SQ. FT.
AREA: 1,500 SQ.FT.
TYPE: GALLERY
INSTALLATION
PROGRAM: EXPERIENTIAL
SPACE
OWNER: SOUTHERN
CALIFORNIA INSTITUTE OF
ARCHITECTURE

Out of Memory for the SCI-Arc Gallery in downtown Los Angeles was an experiential piece: a convergence of sound, material, light, form, and technology. Memory was the vehicle; the familiar was the impetus. The installation proposed a new structural materiality through the use of renewable polyurethane foam as a complete building assembly. Layers of closed cell foam (used structurally) and open cell foam (used acoustically) combined to create it. The pure geometry of the parabola provided a natural self-structural form.

A site-specific composition by world-renowned composer Ken Ueno accompanied the installation. The soundscape explored the spatialization of sound within the gallery, providing an ever-changing mobile, with software designed specifically for the installation. Resonance was exploited in the acoustically absorptive space. Each layer of sound related to an existing environmental sound and reenacted a memory of it. Through experiencing the aestheticized memory of the environmental sounds, one's relationship with them was transformed.

The interior surface of the parabolic structure was a three-dimensional representation of the musical composition. Realized through on-site, six-axis robotic milling, the sonic contours were derived from the sound contained within. A mapping of frequency based on a spectrogram of the composition was translated into points and vectors providing a framework for the digitally modeled three-dimensional surface. The data was then used to robotically carve the volume's interior surface.

The spiraling geometry and acoustically absorptive material magnified both the spatial and the aural. Notions of memory were challenged. Traces of the ambient, combined with visions of the past, present, and future, heightened one's awareness of the space, while altering perceptions. The piece transcended the original vision. The final outcome was derived from the act of making, and the memory of that act was eclipsed by the residual. Only the remnant of our pursuit remained in the gallery afterward.

ACTUAL

TEMPORARY SHORING

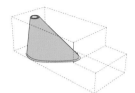

FABRIC FORMWORK

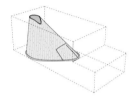

3" CLOSED CELL STRUCTURAL
POLYURETHANE FOAM

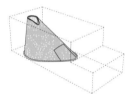

9" OPEN CELL ACOUSTICAL
POLYURETHANE FOAM

6 AXIS ROBOTIC MILLING

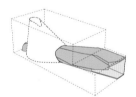

SHADOW PASSAGES

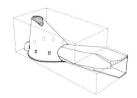

ACOUSTICS AND LIGHTING

SEQUENCING DIAGRAM

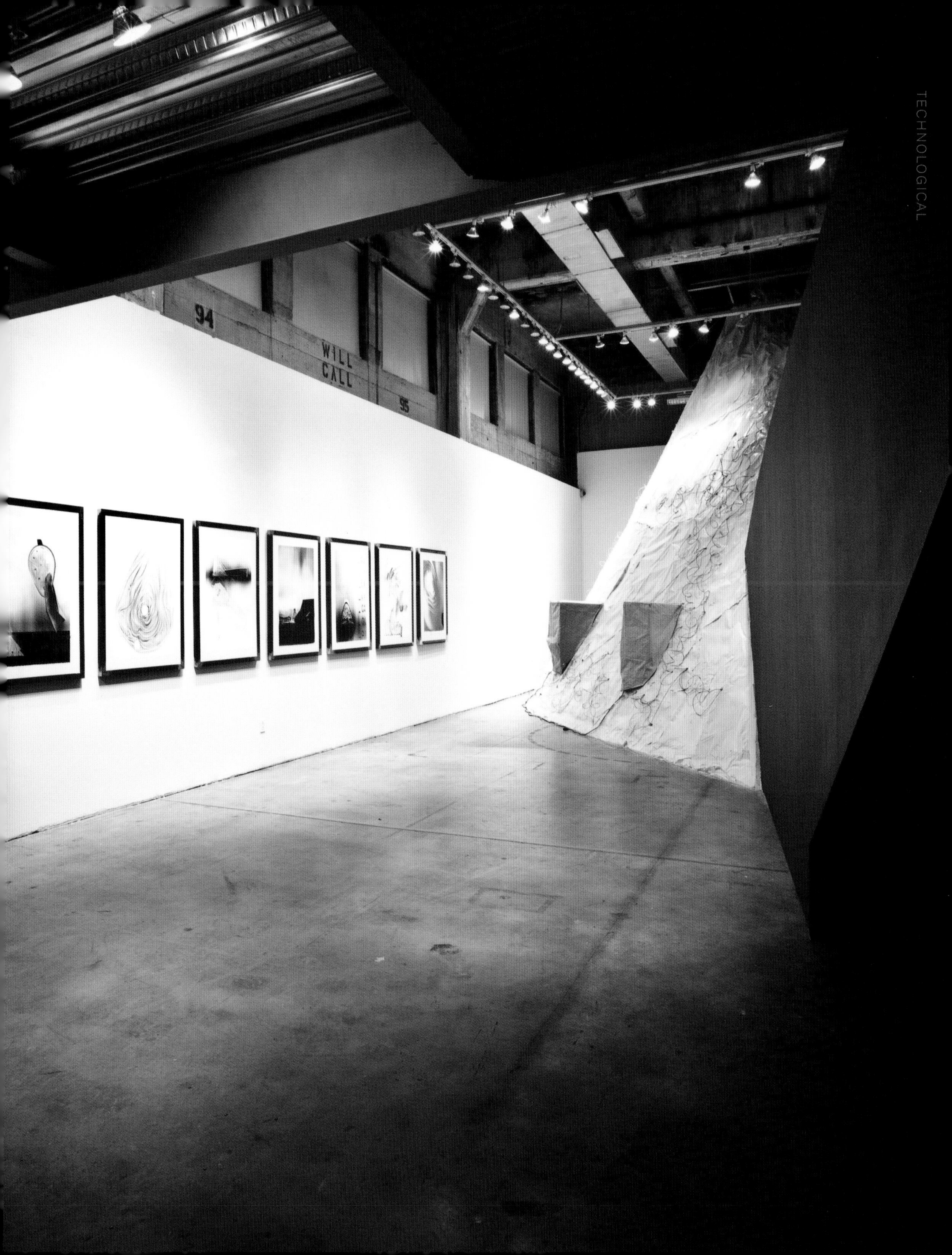
94
WILL
CALL
95

ACTUAL

ROBOTIC TOOLING

ACTUAL

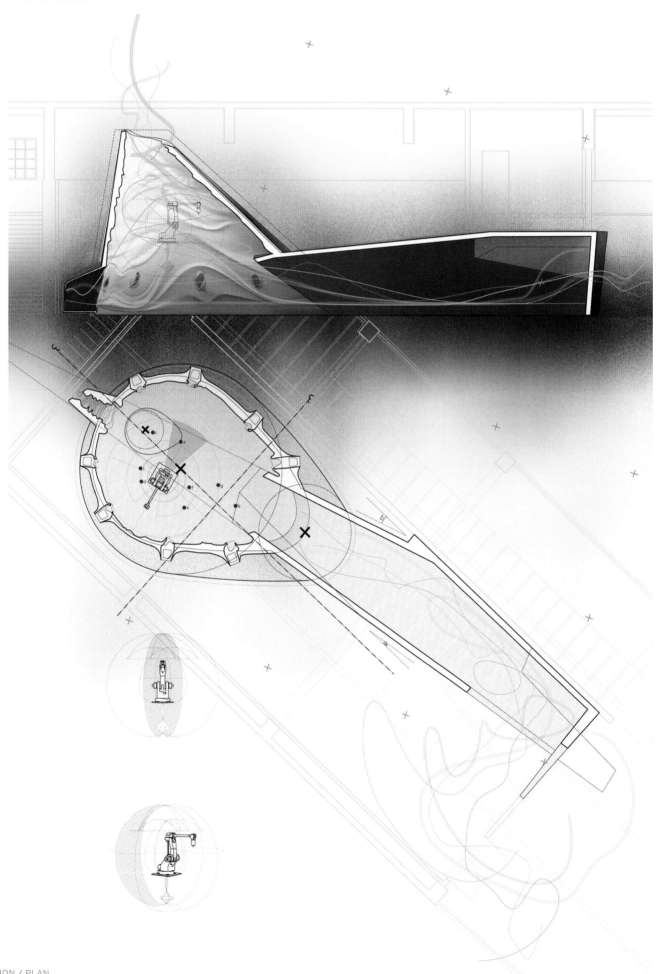

ACTUAL

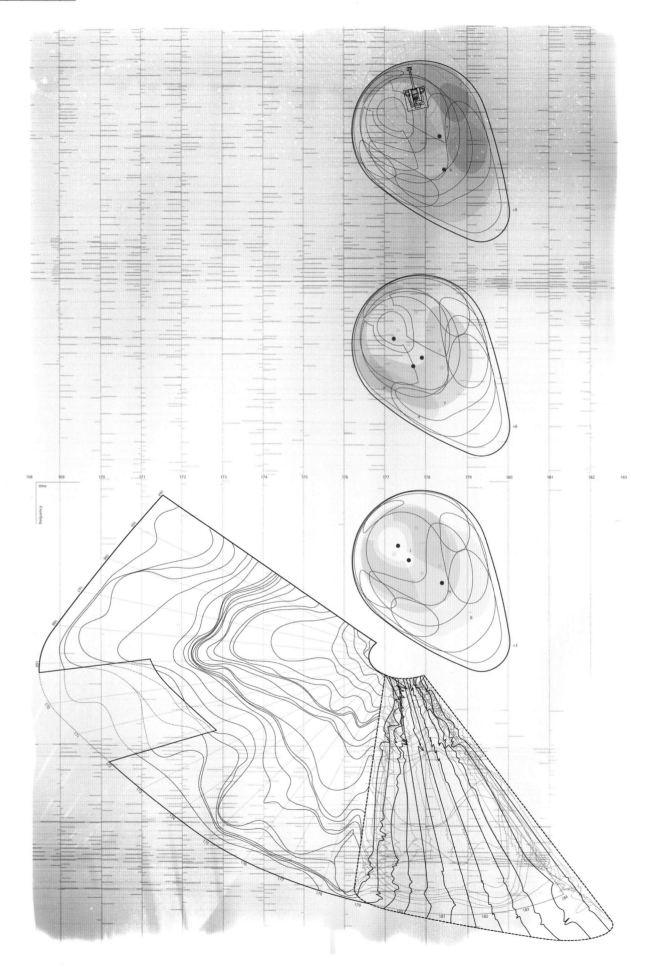

TRANSLATION OF SPECTOGRAM INTO ARTICULATED SURFACE

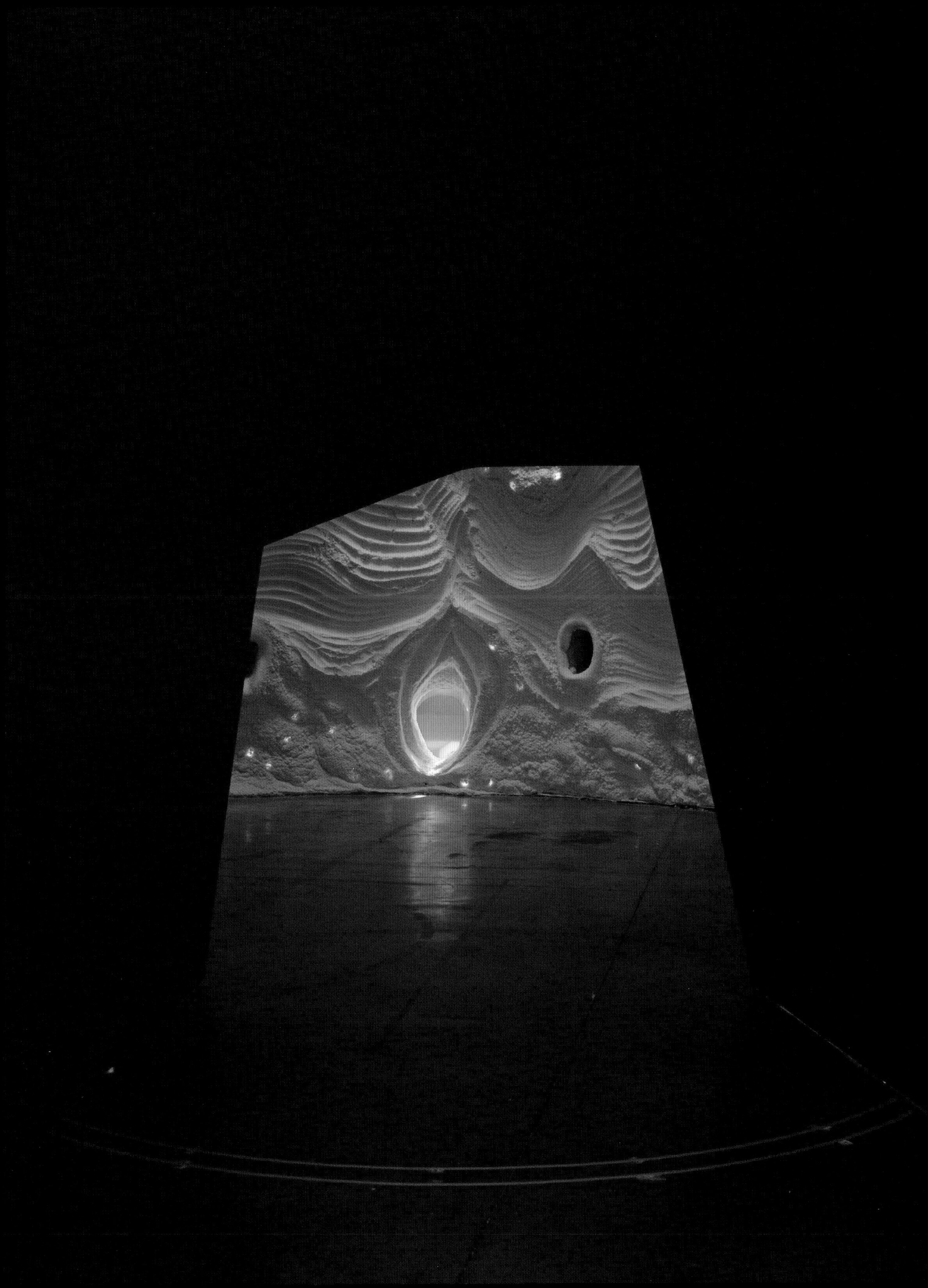

ACTUAL

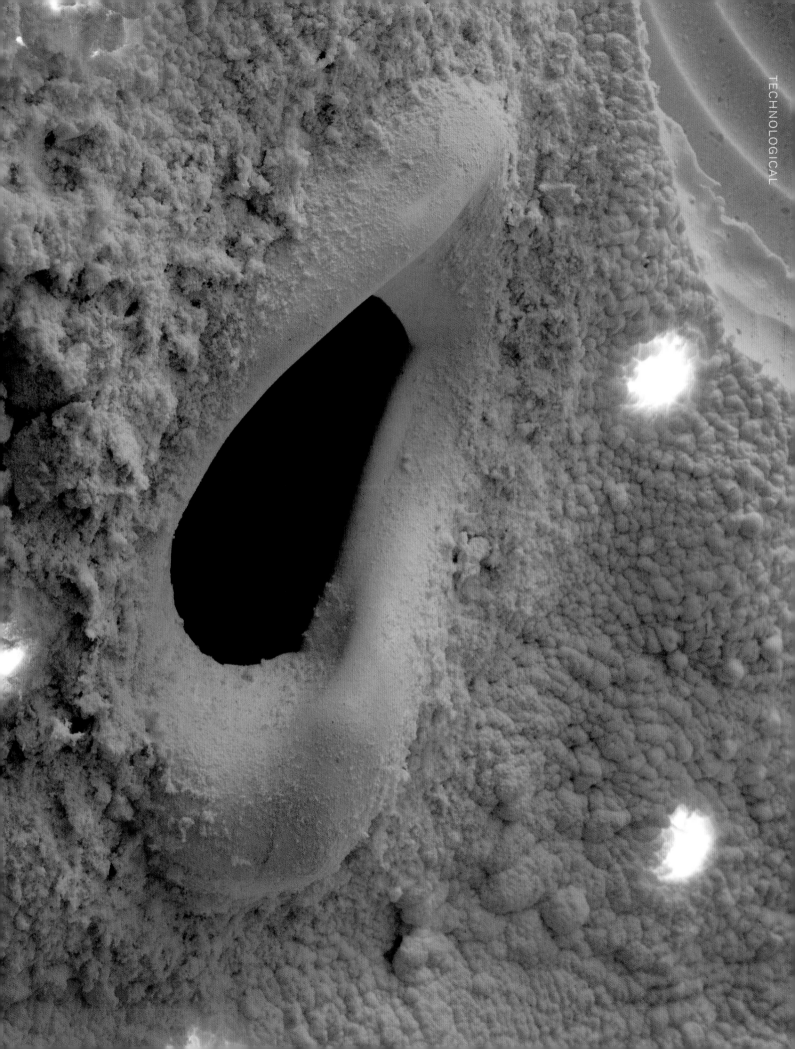

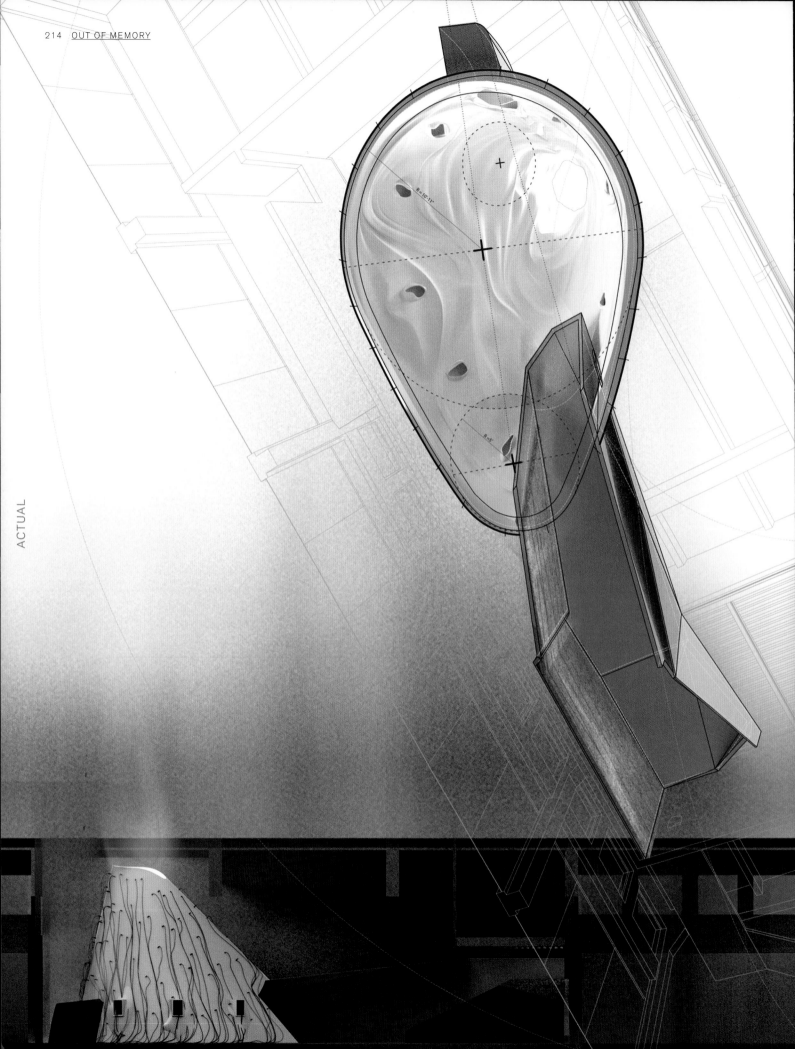

ACTUAL

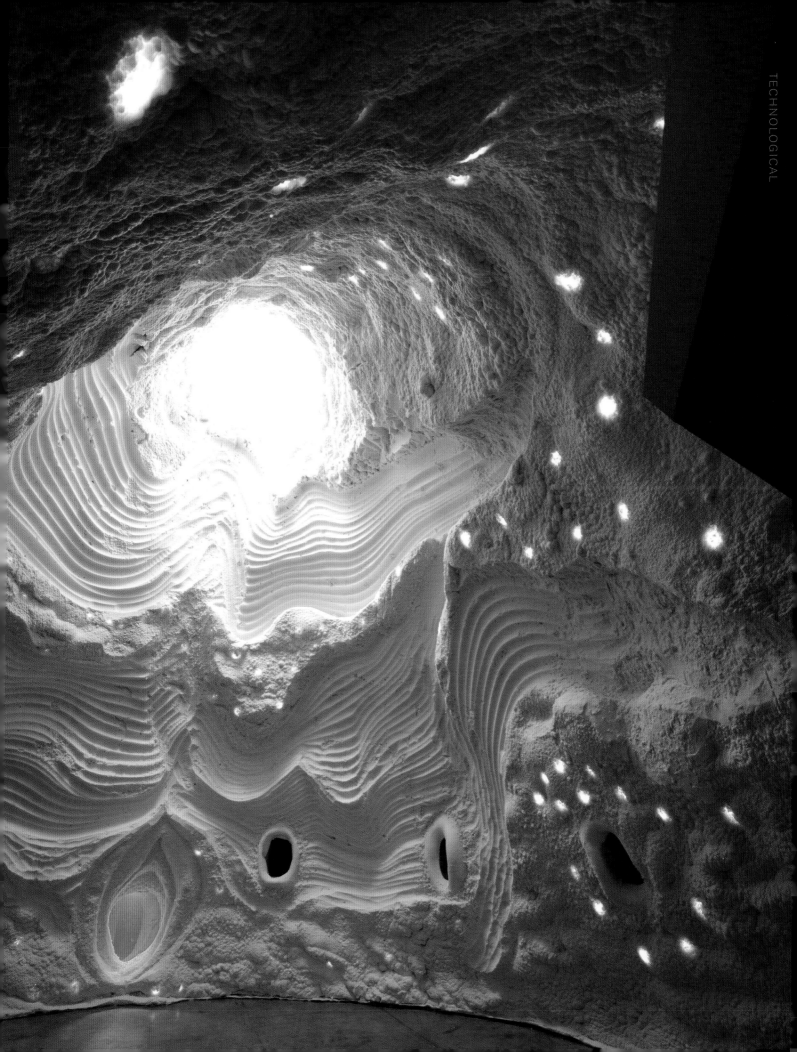

ACTUAL

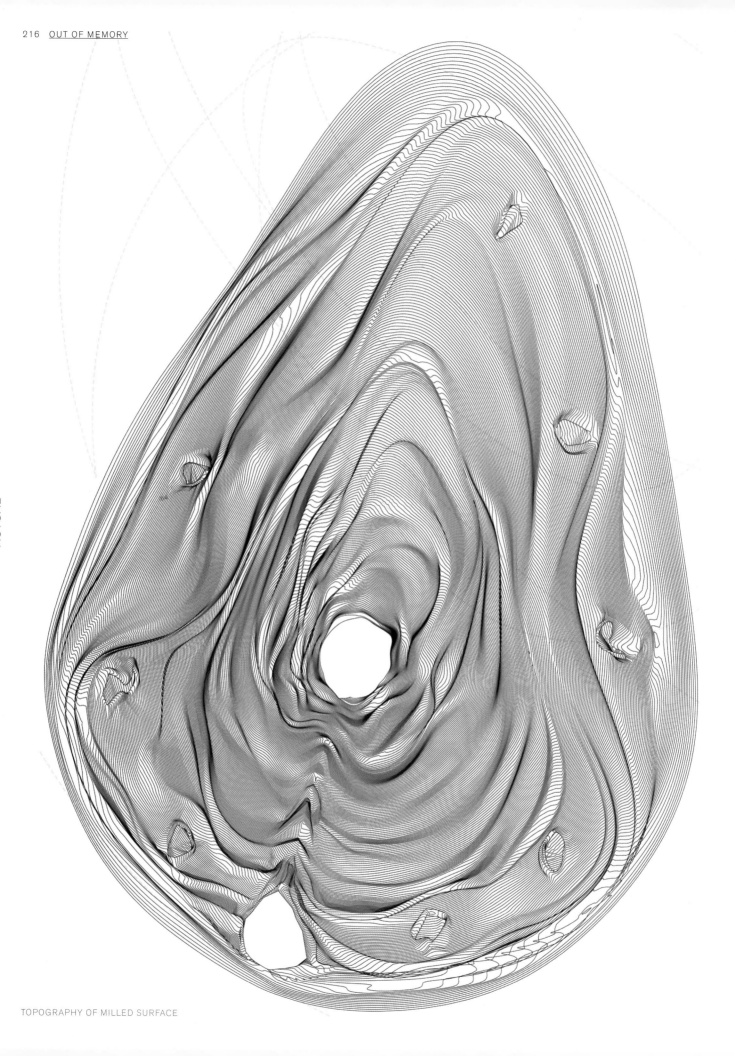

TOPOGRAPHY OF MILLED SURFACE

DIAMOND IN THE ROUGH

KANGDE TOWERS

CHONGQING, CHINA

STATUS: IN DEVELOPMENT
SITE: 6 ACRES
AREA: 1,410,000 SQ.FT.
TYPE: MIXED USE
PROGRAM: COMMERCIAL,
HOTEL, RETAIL,
APARTMENTS
OWNER: KANGDE
CORPORATION

SIMPLE

The Kangde Towers are located in the city of Chongqing, the largest megalopolis in Southwest China. The city's urban core is where the Yangtze and Jialing Rivers meet. The pair of towers will occupy the highest elevation in Jiefangbei, a vital central business and commercial area.

The Kangde Center boasts a maximum density, totaling 1,410,000 square feet. The 46- and 54-story towers rise to 938 feet and are connected at the base with a seven-story building that serves as a plinth. Hotels, residential units, and office space occupy the tower buildings, with commercial and retail at the lower levels. Eighteen floors of subterranean parking is provided.

The city grids are translated into the diagrid fenestration of the buildings, translating into a three-dimensional representation of the city. The lower levels of the building respond to various local conditions and are prominently integrated into the urban fabric of the city center. Seen from a distance and due to their scale, the towers have a dynamic, iconic, and dominant presence along Chongqing's city skyline.

SIMPLE

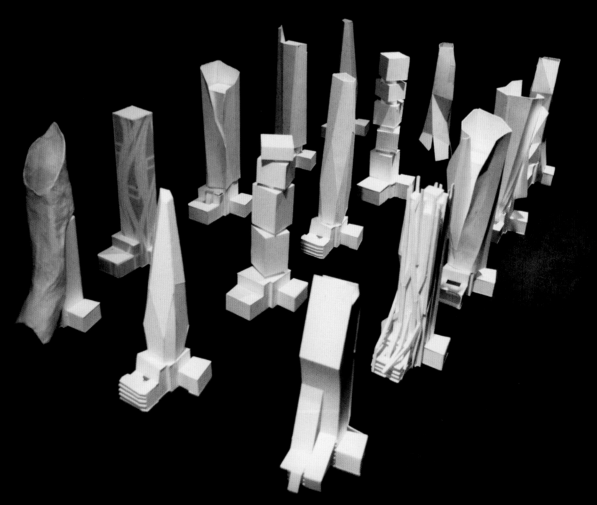

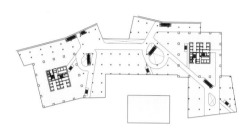

FOURTH LEVEL

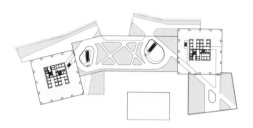

SEVENTH LEVEL

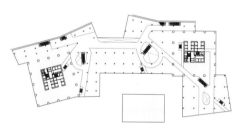

THIRD LEVEL

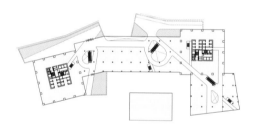

SIXTH LEVEL

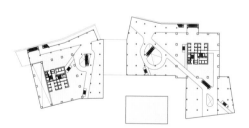

SECOND LEVEL

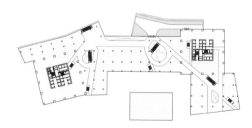

FIFTH LEVEL

SIMPLE

FLOOR PLANS

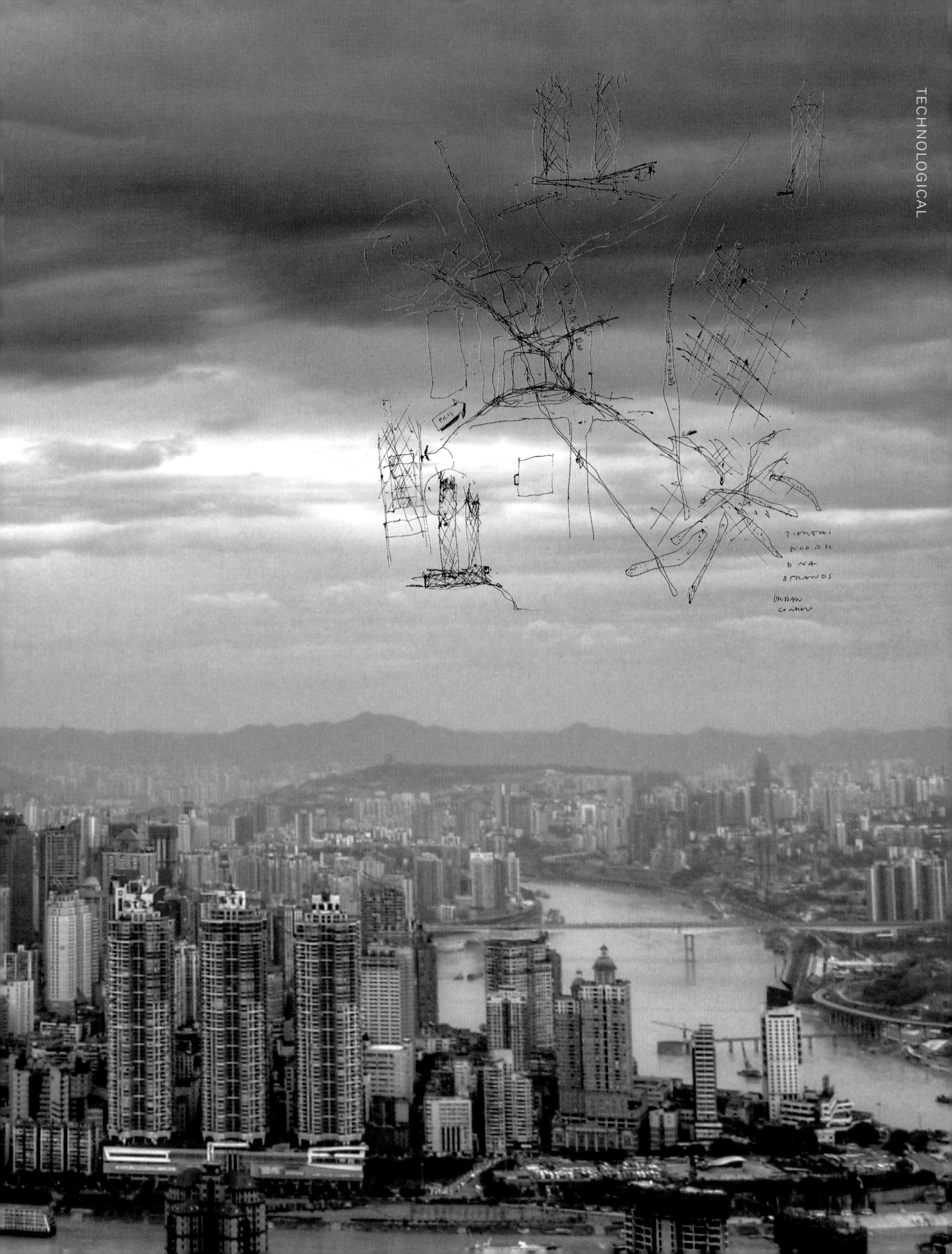

SURFACED

LOTUS VILLA

BEIJING, CHINA

STATUS: IN DEVELOPMENT
SITE: 1.5 ACRES
AREA: 11,000 SQ.FT.
TYPE: RESIDENTIAL
PROGRAM: SINGLE FAMILY
DWELLING
OWNER: JINHAI LAKE LLC

The Lotus Villa is a custom-faceted concrete shell structure nestled into a sloping hillside with a strong connection to Jinhai Lake, Beijing, China. The dynamic form cantilevers out over the water's edge, embracing the lake. The position of the residence on the site reduces the impact of the three-story home on the landscape. The placement, along with the form and massing, optimizes views, while simultaneously maintaining privacy from the street and neighbors.

The architecture represents a 21st-century version of the siheyuan, traditional Chinese courtyard housing, using innovative construction techniques and digital design. The 21st-century siheyuan consists of a series of outdoor rooms that extends the living space of the 11,000-square-foot residence. The courtyards are set along the north-south axis. Water is the connective tissue that ties the outdoor spaces back to the lake. Each courtyard has its own distinct characteristics defined by a unique water element. The entrance court features a serene koi pond and

garden, serving as a place for contemplation. The central atrium gallery has a vibrant water fountain that is experienced from everywhere in the house. The lakeside terrace contains a long linear reflecting pool extending into the lake. Finally, the lower-level terrace is a continuation of the interior space and surrounds the 50-foot-long pool that continues out over the water's edge.

The central atrium is the heart of the home. Like the lotus, the structural core rises from the land, symbolically representing an inward focus while at the same time providing an outward splendor. The core serves as the internal structural system and the main circulation for the house. Diffused light filters through the structural filigree illuminating all levels of the residence. The branching structure is a networked grid, and the structural strands at the lower levels gradually become the surface of the building envelope.

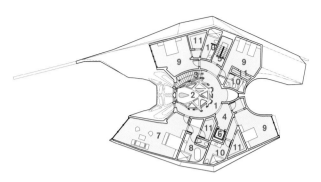

SECOND LEVEL
1. ATRIUM GALLERY **2.** WATER GARDEN **3.** GRAND STAIRS **4.** VESTIBULE **5.** SERVICE STAIRS
6. ELEVATOR **7.** MASTER BEDROOM **8.** MASTER BATHROOM **9.** BEDROOM **10.** BATHROOM **11.** CLOSET

ACTUAL

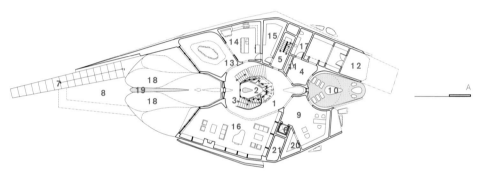

GROUND LEVEL
1. ATRIUM GALLERY **2.** WATER GARDEN **3.** GRAND STAIRS **4.** VESTIBULE **5.** SERVICE STAIRS
6. ELEVATOR **7.** EXTERIOR STAIRS **8.** POOL **9.** STUDY / LIBRARY **10.** FRONT COURTYARD / KOI
POND **11.** CLOSET **12.** ENTRY **13.** DINING ROOM **14.** KITCHEN **15.** PANTRY **16.** LIVING AREA
17. POWDER ROOM **18.** TERRACE **19.** STORAGE **20.** REFLECTING POOL **21.** MECHANICAL SHAFT

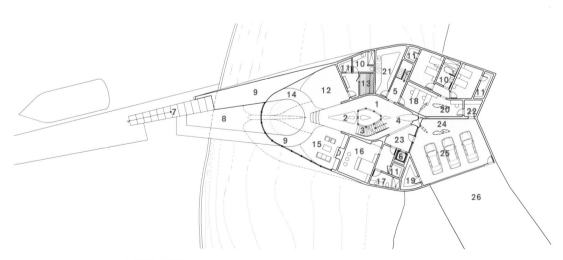

LOWER LEVEL
1. ATRIUM GALLERY **2.** WATER GARDEN **3.** GRAND STAIRS **4.** VESTIBULE **5.** SERVICE STAIRS
6. ELEVATOR **7.** EXTERIOR STAIR **8.** POOL **9.** INDOOR / OUTDOOR **10.** BATHROOM **11.** CLOSET
12. CHANGING ROOM **13.** SAUNA **14.** WORKOUT AREA **15.** FAMILY ROOM **16.** GUEST BEDROOM
17. GUEST BATHROOM **18.** SERVANT'S QUARTERS **19.** STORAGE **20.** SERVANT'S WORK AREA
21. LAUNDRY ROOM **22.** CHAUFFEUR STATION **23.** RESIDENT'S ENTRY **24.** SERVANT'S ENTRY
25. GARAGE **26.** DRIVEWAY

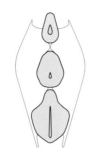

COURTYARD / WATER ELEMENTS

ACTUAL

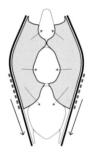

PRIVACY

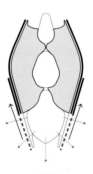

VIEW

COURTYARD STRUCTURE TO SURFACE TRANSITION

ACTUAL

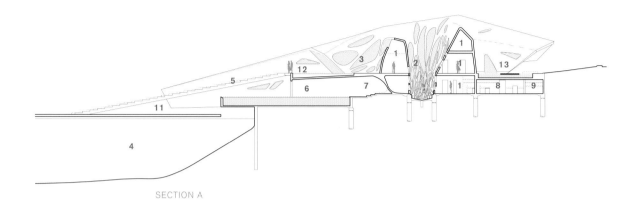

SECTION A

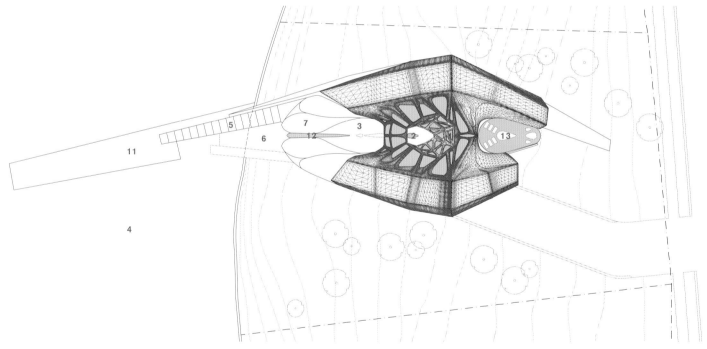

SITE PLAN

1. ATRIUM GALLERY 2. WATER GARDEN 3. EXTERIOR COURT 4. LAKE 5. EXTERIOR STAIRS
6. POOL 7. INDOOR / OUTDOOR TERRACE 8. SERVANT'S WORK AREA 9. CHAUFFEUR STATION
10. ENTRY 11. DOCK 12. REFLECTING POOL 13. ENTRY COURT / KOI POND

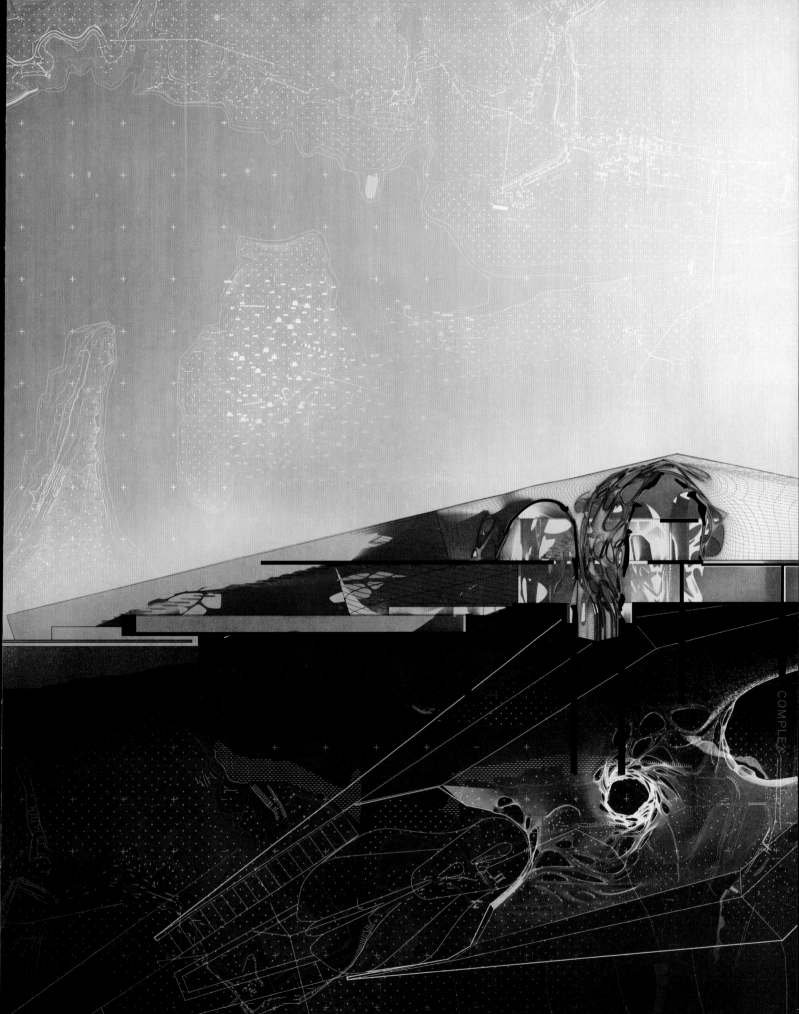

MANUFACTURED

NATURE GIRL

LOUDERMILK ON MELROSE

WEST HOLLYWOOD,
CALIFORNIA

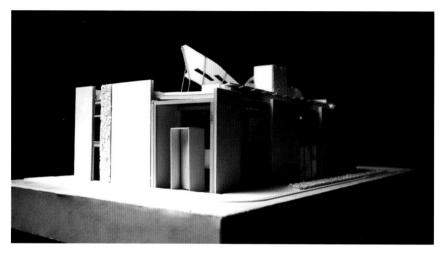

STATUS: BUILT 2008
SITE: 6,200 SQ.FT.
AREA: 4,200 SQ.FT.
TYPE: RETAIL
PROGRAM: BOUTIQUE,
GALLERY, CAFÉ
OWNER: LINDA
LOUDERMILK

The 4,200-square-foot building on Melrose Avenue in Los Angeles is the flagship showroom for eco-fashionista Linda Loudermilk. The designer's philosophy of celebrating elements found in nature, while flattering the natural movement of the body, is carried through to the building's architecture. Nature is the core of the design in both the retail environment and the fine couture in the designer's line.

The program consists of retail space at the ground level and executive offices located on the upper level. The two-story showroom serves as a backdrop for the collection. A separate salon is provided for private showings and fittings. The space under the main stair is the focal point of the lower level, a transparent shell that functions as a dressing pod. It informs and is informed by a cast fiberglass shell that allows it

to be freestanding. Throughout the design process, new materials were researched for use, and state-of-the-art fabrication techniques were employed. Using the dressing pod as an example, the free-form shape resembles something found in nature, but its fabrication and material reveal an artificial simulation.

The project is a showcase for sustainable building systems, products, and methods of construction. The rooftop garden is an extension of the landscape. A solar canopy provides shelter for the deck, while simultaneously providing power for the building. Environmentally mindful building systems, such as reclaimed, recycled, rapidly renewable materials, and solar technology are some of the components used to meet LEED certification criteria.

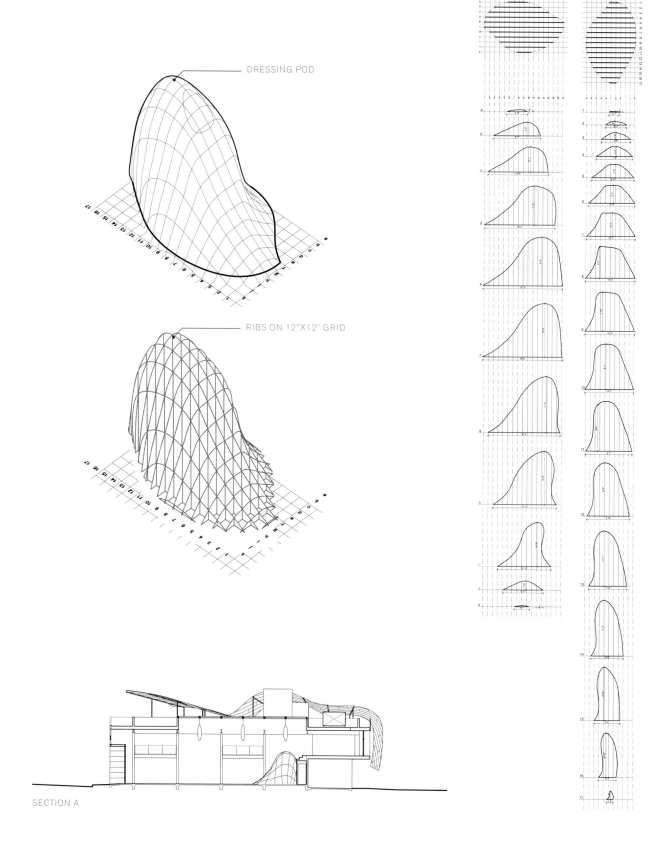

DRESSING POD

RIBS ON 12"X12" GRID

SECTION A

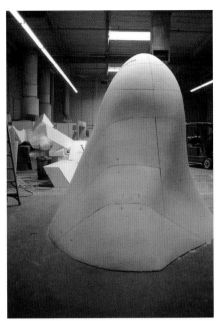

MANUFACTURED

AN ICON REINVISIONED

SIAM(EAMES) CHAIR

LOS ANGELES, CALIFORNIA

STATUS: BUILT 2014

DIMENSIONS: 34" X 34"

TYPE: FURNITURE

PROGRAM: RE-IMAGINE EAMES CHAIR

OWNER: ADOBE

The Siam(eames) Twin Chair reintroduces the iconic, molded fiberglass chair designed by Ray and Charles Eames in 1957. The once ubiquitous, mass-produced chair is re-envisioned as a custom fabricated piece. In their work, the Eameses coupled the latest technologies with the use of new and innovative materials.

The shell chair was a product of their comprehensive creative process typified by cross-pollination, including borrowing fabrication techniques and materials from diverse disciplines. If Ray and Charles were alive today, it is assumed they would be fascinated by the infinite possibilities that result when emergent technologies are combined with the most advanced methods of fabrication, as they were by the most up-to-date technology of their time.

In the case of the reinterpreted version of the chair, technology is used to robotically emblazon a quintessential Eames pattern onto the shells. The six-axis robotic milling allows for a precise cut of the shells' complex shapes making it possible for two pieces to become one. The shells are then mirrored along the vertical axis and conjoined, creating a bilaterally symmetrical composition. Through a process of division and multiplication, aided by technology, a new chair is born from a design nearly 60 years old.

The 21st-century design inspires renewed appreciation for the original chair. When the curves of the chair are paired with the twin, the molded chair maintains its form, while establishing a new relationship with the body (or bodies). This type of manipulation of form keeps with the Eames' predilection for experimentation with furniture. In their creative process, they too welcomed and embraced contradictions.

MANUFACTURED

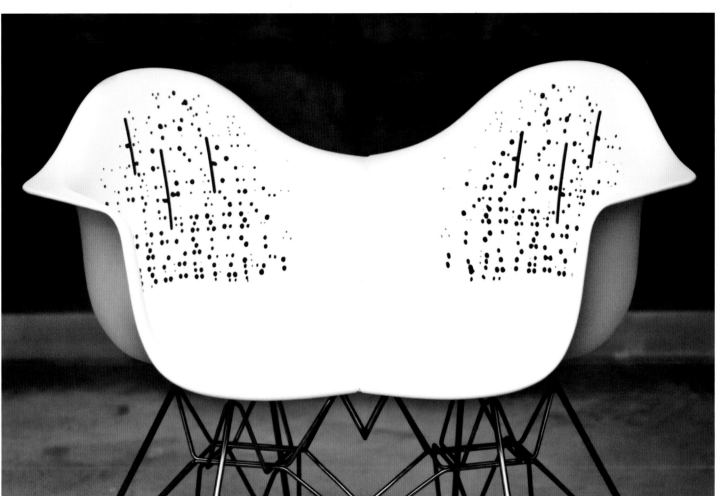

MANUFACTURED

FIGURAL BLUR

ADOBE HQ

SAN JOSE, CALIFORNIA

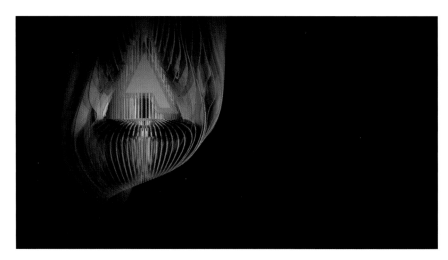

STATUS: BUILT 2014
DIMENSIONS: 18"X18"X36"
TYPE: ENVIRONMENTAL
PROGRAM: LIGHTING
OWNER: ADOBE

Adobe asked us to re-imagine their logo. We were immediately struck by its boldness, simplicity, and strength. Adobe represents and facilitates creativity, which immediately focused our exploration. What would happen if we began to transform the triangular icon? What if we eliminated all the angles and softened the edges? What if a new complex geometry emerged from the primitive form?

We were interested in the interplay between the hard and soft. Through a series of digital manipulations, the angles and sharp edges gradually disappeared, and the logo became more pliant and malleable. We decided to partially obscure it by burying it inside a network of lines, more specifically 100 blades of glass radiating from the central core, nesting the original logo. The viewer must look closely to see the brand in a new way.

It was our desire to make more than a mere artifact. The interplay of light and shadow creates atmospheric effects. The logo becomes the site where the Adobe brand is projected and takes on new meaning. By encouraging "new ways of seeing," the Adobe mark reflects the creativity that inspired us and allows that creativity to shine through.

MANUFACTURED

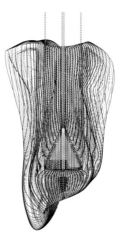

FRONT ELEVATION

SIDE ELEVATION

BACK ELEVATION

ELEVATIONS

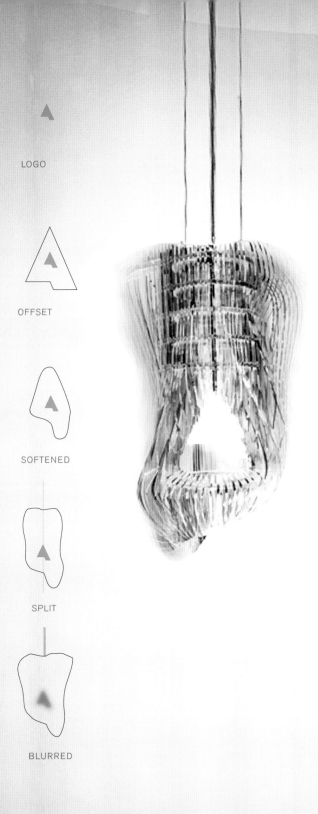

LOGO

OFFSET

SOFTENED

SPLIT

BLURRED

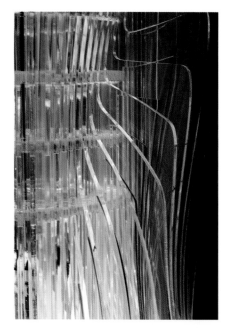
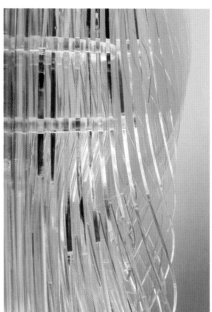

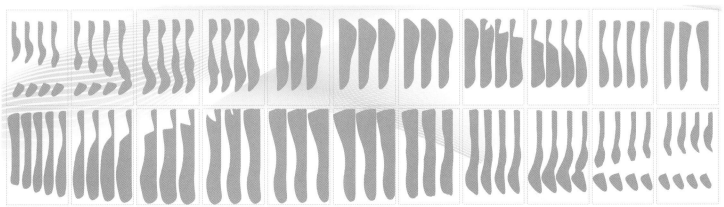

CONJOINED

TWIN

NATURAL

JINHAI LAKE, CHINA

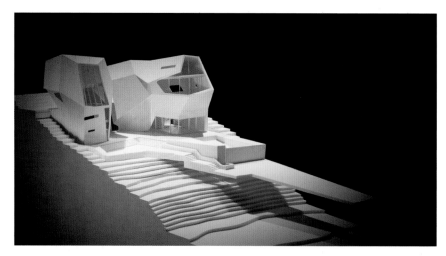

STATUS: IN DEVELOPMENT
SITE: 2 ACRES
AREA: 10,200 SQ.FT.
TYPE: RESIDENTIAL
PROGRAM: MULTIFAMILY
DWELLING
OWNER: PRIVATE

The Twin villa is located 60 miles outside Beijing, in the Pinggu District of China, in a new residential and leisure development abutting an artificial lake. The farming community has been enhanced by the addition of a village center and farmworker housing. Market-rate housing has been introduced with a mix for seniors, moderate-income duplexes, and villas. Existing hospitality services are expanding, and public access to the lake is increasing. Numerous leisure activities are available, including boating and golf.

The topography of the island site is fairly steep. The level of the lake varies depending on rainfall during the rainy season, rendering a portion of the lot, adjacent to the water, unbuildable. A pair of monolithic columns contributes to the Twin villa's dynamic form. Custom-faceted concrete shell structures are nestled into the sloping hillside, cantilevering over the downslope, reaching out toward the lake. By embedding the semi-subterranean building into the earth, the villa's

impact on the landscape is reduced. The siting of the residence and its form and massing optimize views, while simultaneously maintaining privacy from the street and neighbors.

Two wings function as the primary structural system, supporting the villa's primary circulation. A central circulation spine separates the pair of residential volumes. The interstitial space is a transparent threshold that functions as a visual connector to the lake. Diffused light filters through the transparent void, illuminating all levels of the home. Concrete is the region's predominant building material and preferred choice of local craftspeople, so various applications of the versatile material are used throughout, expanding its potential. Notions of fluidity, porosity, thickness, and smoothness are explored in regard to the relationship between the interior surfaces and the exterior building volume.

SECOND LEVEL
1. GRAND STAIRS **2.** MASTER BEDROOM SUITE I **3.** MASTER BATHROOM I **4.** MASTER CLOSET I
5. MASTER BALCONY I **6.** MASTER BEDROOM SUITE II **7.** MASTER BATHROOM II **8.** MASTER
CLOSET II **9.** MASTER BALCONY II **10.** BEDROOM **11.** BATHROOM **12.** ELEVATOR **13.** SERVICE
STAIRS **14.** STORAGE

NATURAL

GROUND LEVEL
1. ENTRY **2.** GRAND STAIRS **3.** FORMAL LIVING ROOM **4.** FORMAL BALCONY **5.** BEDROOM
6. BATHROOM **7.** POWDER ROOM **8.** KITCHEN **9.** DINING ROOM **10.** FAMILY ROOM
11. LIBRARY **12.** FAMILY BALCONY **13.** ELEVATOR **14.** SERVICE KITCHEN **15.** PANTRY
16. SERVICE STAIRS **17.** STORAGE **18.** CLOSET **19.** DRIVEWAY

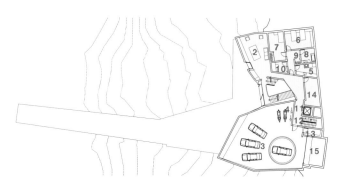

-1 LEVEL
1. GRAND STAIRS **2.** DEN/GAMES ROOM **3.** GARAGE **4.** BICYCLE / MOTORCYCLE STORAGE
5. LAUNDRY ROOM **6.** SERVANT'S BEDROOM **7.** CHAUFFEUR'S BEDROOM **8.** BATHROOM
9. CLOSET **10.** WORK ROOM **11.** ELEVATOR **12.** SERVICE STAIRS **13.** STORAGE
14. MECHANICAL **15.** GARAGE RAMP

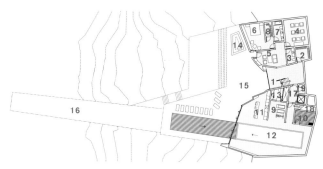

-2 LEVEL
1. GRAND STAIRS **2.** WINE CELLAR **3.** POWDER ROOM **4.** MOVIE ROOM **5.** DEN **6.** GUEST
BEDROOM **7.** GUEST BATHROOM **8.** CLOSET **9.** GYM **10.** SAUNA **11.** BAR **12.** POOL **13.** BATH-
ROOM **14.** JACUZZI **15.** DECK **16.** DOCK **17.** ELEVATOR **18.** SERVICE STAIRS **19.** STORAGE

NATURAL

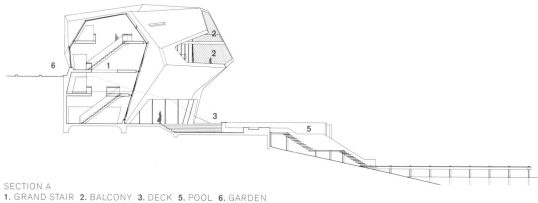

SECTION A
1. GRAND STAIR 2. BALCONY 3. DECK 5. POOL 6. GARDEN

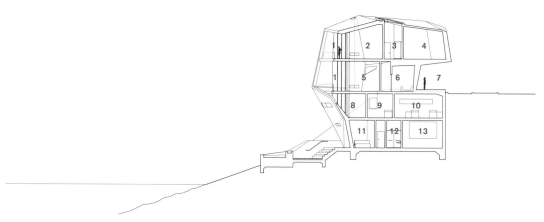

SECTION B
1. BALCONY 2. MASTER BEDROOM SUITE 3. MASTER BATHROOM 4. MASTER CLOSET 5. FORMAL
LIVING ROOM 6. BEDROOM 7. GARDEN 8. DEN/GAMES ROOM 9. CHAUFFEUR'S BEDROOM
10. SERVANT'S BEDROOM 11. GUEST BEDROOM 12. GUEST BATHROOM 13. MOVIE ROOM

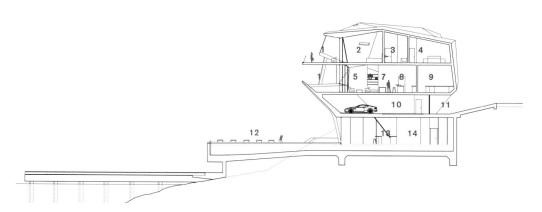

SECTION C
1. BALCONY 2. MASTER BEDROOM SUITE 3. MASTER BATHROOM 4. BEDROOM 5. FAMILY ROOM
6. LIBRARY 7. DINING ROOM 8. KITCHEN 9. SERVICE KITCHEN 10. GARAGE 11. DRIVEWAY
12. POOL 13. BAR 14. INDOOR POOL

NATURAL

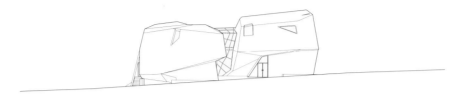

SOUTH ELEVATION

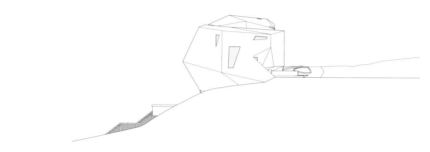

EAST ELEVATION

NORTH ELEVATION

ELEVATIONS

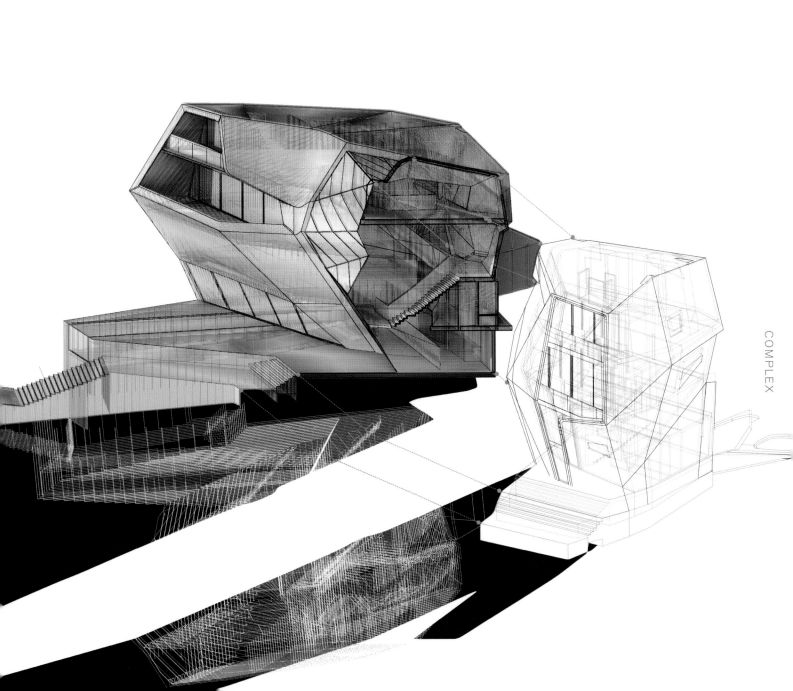

BRANCHED

NATURAL

VILLA FOR HIS HIGHNESS
SHEIKH SULTAN BIN ZAYED AL NAHYAN

SKHIRAT, MOROCCO

STATUS: IN DEVELOPMENT
SITE: 21 ACRES
AREA: 5,200 SQ.FT.
TYPE: MIXED USE
PROGRAM: HOUSING,
GUEST QUARTERS,
CONFERENCE CENTER
OWNER: HIS HIGHNESS
SHEIKH SULTAN BIN ZAYED
AL NAHYAN

Located at the northernmost tip of Africa, where the desert meets the Atlantic Ocean, the Villa Skhirat is a sustainable, site-specific series of building components strategically placed within a spectacular seaside Moroccan landscape. The project is designed as a continuation of the strata of the site.

Inspiration came from our client's love of the Atlas cedar tree, a symbol of immortality, purity, and cleansing. The strength and structural logic of the tree were catalysts for creating the natural forms of the reinforced concrete building.

The branch-like structure is translated into strands that become surfaces. These strands are heavy and grounded firmly, embedded into the landscape, and become increasingly lighter as the system rises and the necessity for the structure diminishes. The reinforced concrete and the natural form of the tree are entwined in the design and in its genesis.

The fragmented structure at the top of the building serves as an armature to support the skylight. The structural filigree filters ever-changing mosaics of light that illuminate the interior surfaces of the main building. These light patterns change throughout the day and from season to season. The building skin exhibits various degrees of transparency and porosity—the result of investigating notions of privacy and exposure.

Apertures in the building envelope facilitate natural ventilation. A layering of exterior surfaces incorporates an environmentally mindful building approach providing both heat and sun protection. The protected inner courtyard is framed by several building components. Various public and private entities intertwine creating distinct circulation paths.

While the structural network that becomes the surface of the building is based on a geometry inspired by nature, and natural forms are a significant factor in the project's inception, they are translated in the digital design process. Through material selection, they blend into the innovative structural system for this contemporary residence.

NATURAL

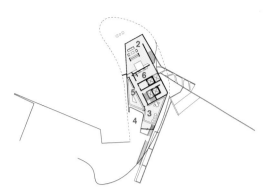

THIRD LEVEL
1. BEDROOM 2. LIVING ROOM 3. LIBRARY 4. TERRACE 5. DRESSING 6. BATHROOM

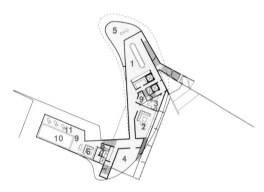

SECOND LEVEL
1. DINING ROOM 2. MEDIA ROOM 3. PREP. KITCHEN / PANTRY 4. TERRACE 5. COVERED WALKWAY
6. POOL HOUSE 7. BATHROOM 8. KITCHEN 9. PATIO 10. POOL 11. COURTYARD GARDEN

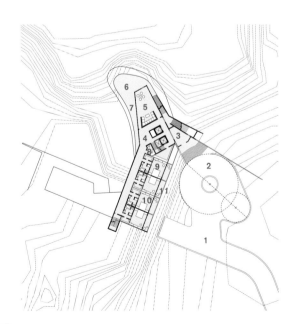

GROUND LEVEL
1. DRIVEWAY 2. MOTOR COURT 3. ENTRY 4. FOYER 5. TERRACE 6. RECEPTION 7. PATIO
8. POWDER ROOM 9. GUEST BEDROOM 10. GUEST BEDROOM 11. GUEST DECK

NATURAL

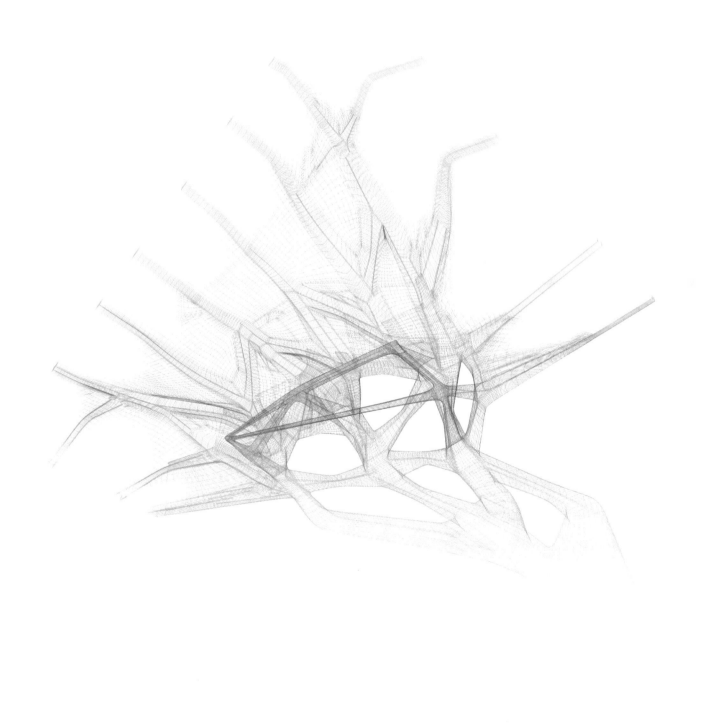

STRUCTURAL DIAGRAM / ELEVATION

WRAPSODY IN WHITE

MONTEE KARP

PACIFIC PALISADES,
CALIFORNIA

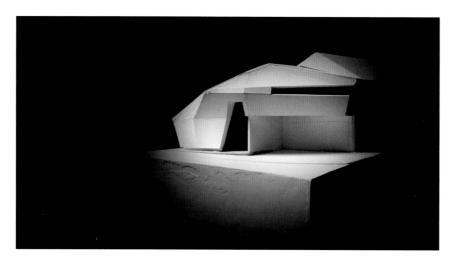

STATUS: BUILT 2014
SITE: 16,000 SQ.FT.
AREA: 2,200 SQ.FT.
TYPE: RESIDENTIAL
PROGRAM: SINGLE FAMILY
DWELLING
OWNER: NINA MONTEE
AND DR. HARVEY KARP

The 2,200-square-foot residence is located on a hillside site in Malibu, California with panoramic views of the Pacific Ocean. The existing post-and-beam home in need of structural, programmatic, and environmental upgrades was re-envisioned for the 21st century.

The existing roof geometry is accentuated creating a language of faceted surfaces. A grand entry door fabricated with a stainless steel tube frame marks the threshold into the relatively small house. The 10-foot-high door makes use of a hydraulic pivot and concealed magnetic locking device. The articulated volume of the building's front façade extends indoors to define the interior spaces, resulting in a dematerialization of the roof, wall, and floor planes, framing the extraordinary views of Santa Monica Bay.

The minimalist, gallery-like, interior living space is designed to accommodate our client's extensive collection of contemporary art. Display niches, lighting, and spatial configurations are all intended to enhance the experience of viewing and interacting with the artwork. Each of the stair's cantilevering steel treads has a custom laser-cut pattern. The skylight filters light through the perforated stair, projecting an ever-changing texture of shadow and light, enlivening the walls and floor. The perforations, hollow stairs (evident from below), and missing handrail (facing the living space) make the stairwell appear to float in space. A half-height glass wall, surrounding the landing at the top of the stair, underscores this effect.

Sustainable features are integral to the design and include elements such as a 5-kilowatt photovoltaic system. Solar power is linked to a charging station in the garage for an electric vehicle. Terrazzo flooring contains hydronic radiant heating and energy-efficient building systems. A sustainable material palette is used throughout.

SECOND LEVEL

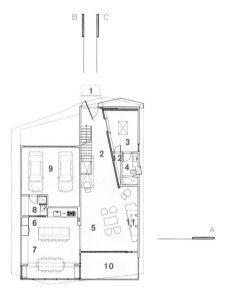

GROUND LEVEL

1. ENTRANCE 2. GALLERY 3. LIBRARY 4. BATHROOM 5. LIVING ROOM 6. KITCHEN
7. DINING ROOM 8. LAUNDRY ROOM 9. GARAGE 10. TERRACE 11. FIREPLACE 12. CLOSET
13. BEDROOM 14. OFFICE

MANUFACTURED

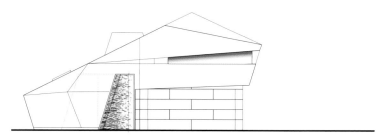

NORTH ELEVATION

ELEVATION

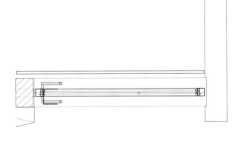

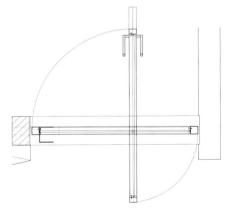

MANUFACTURED

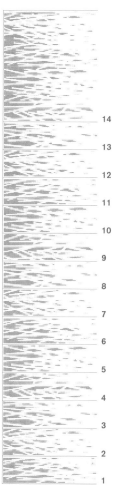

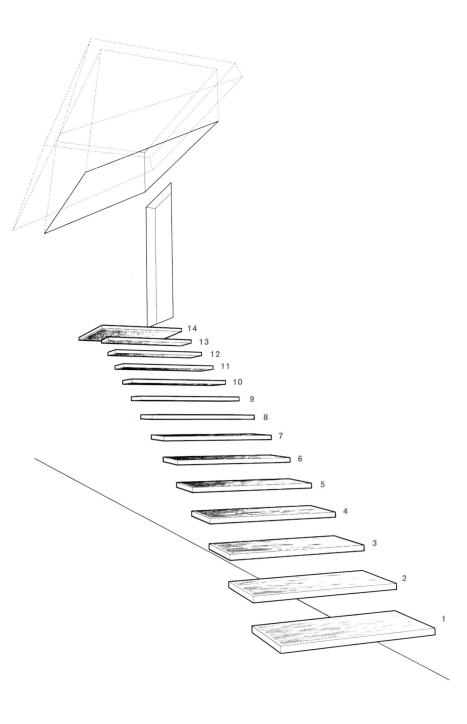

STAIR PERSPECTIVE / PLAN

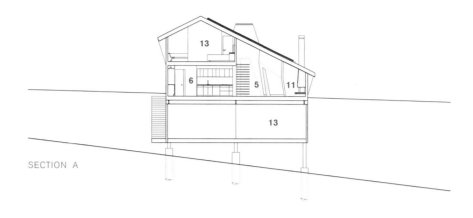

SECTION A

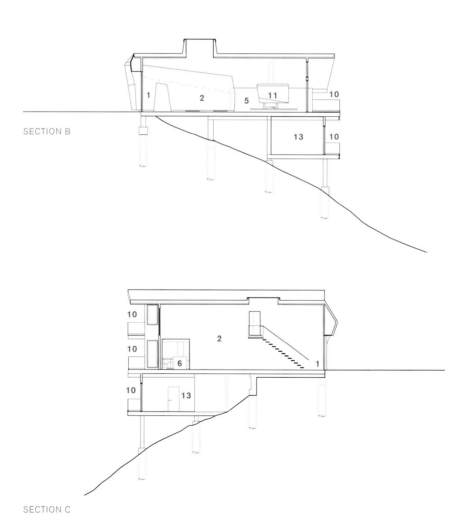

SECTION B

SECTION C

1. ENTRANCE **2.** GALLERY **3.** LIBRARY **4.** BATHROOM **5.** LIVING ROOM **6.** KITCHEN
7. DINING ROOM **8.** LAUNDRY ROOM **9.** GARAGE **10.** TERRACE **11.** FIREPLACE **12.** CLOSET
13. BEDROOM **14.** OFFICE

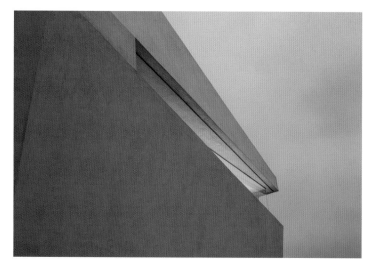

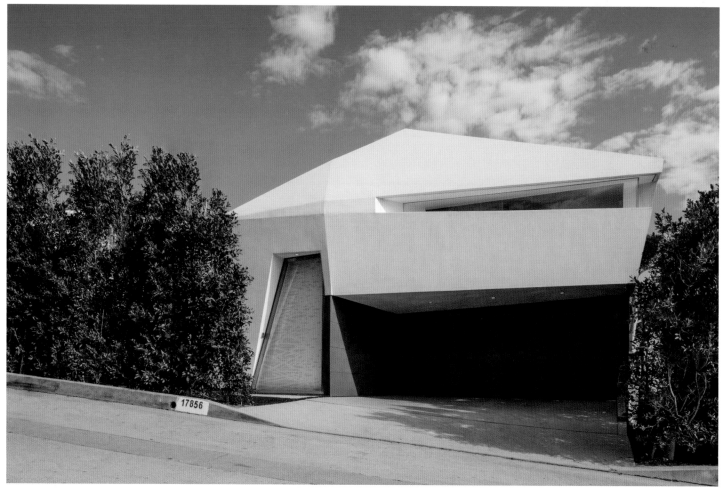

DIGITAL

MANUFACTURED

NEW ANCIENT

RICK OWENS/SELFRIDGES

LONDON, ENGLAND

STATUS: BUILT 2014
SITE: SELFRIDGES DEPT
STORE
AREA: 1,200 SQ.FT.
TYPE: RETAIL
PROGRAM: MEN'S SHOP
OWNER: RICK OWENS CORP

The Rick Owens shop is located within one of the most desirable shopping destinations in the world, Selfridges Department Store on Oxford Street in London. We worked closely with fashion designer Rick Owens and his team to create the custom environment. Extensive research was conducted into surface treatments inspired by the designer's ongoing interest in raw and tactile materials, combined with technologically advanced fabrication techniques.

The interior is inspired by the opera *Salome* by Richard Strauss, a longtime muse of the designer. Highly articulated white walls hold the designer's distinct work. The surfaces are a three-dimensional representation of a musical composition. Realized through six-axis robotic milling, the sonic contours were derived from the musical score. A spectrogram of the composition served as a source from which a mapping of frequency was translated into points and vectors. This provided a framework for the digitally modeled three-dimensional surface. The data was then used to robotically carve the interior surfaces.

The white textured walls offer a distinct visual enclosure. The contrast of the two foam treatments and the natural raw foam, alongside robotically milled foam, offers a counterpoint that is in alignment with the philosophy of the influential designer.

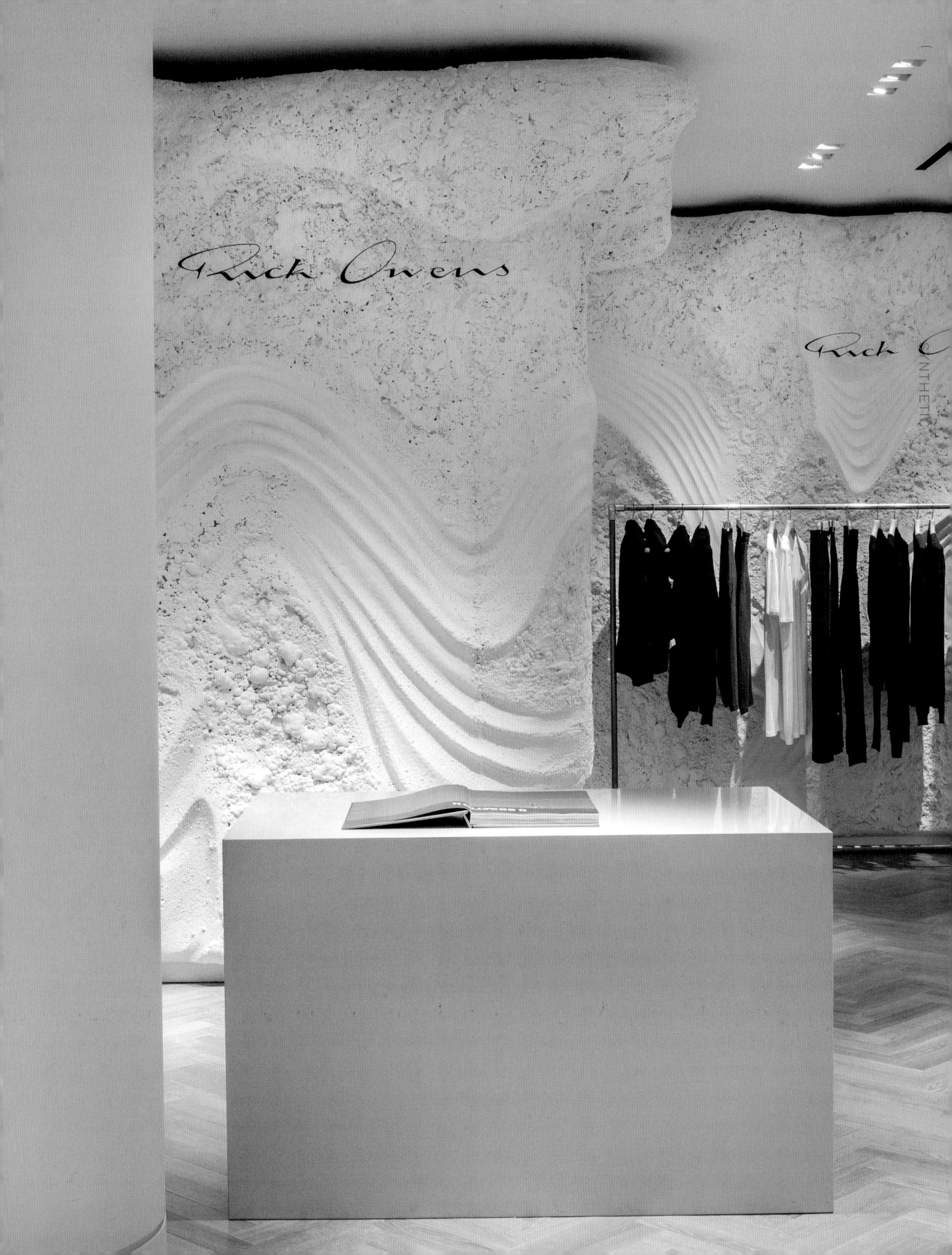
Rick Owens

MANUFACTURED

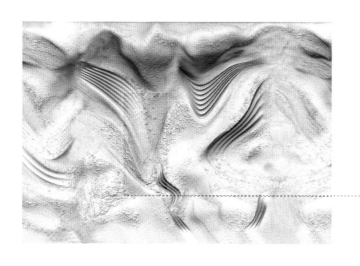

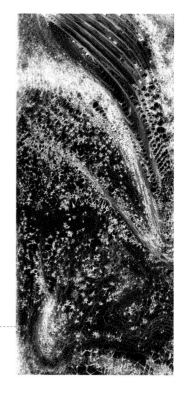

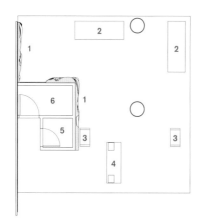

1. ARTICULATED SURFACE **2.** DISPLAY **3.** BENCH **4.** CASH DESK **5.** FITTING ROOM **6.** STOCKROOM

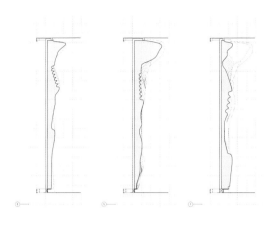

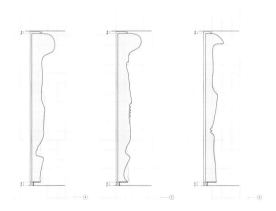

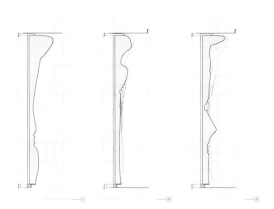

WALL SECTIONS

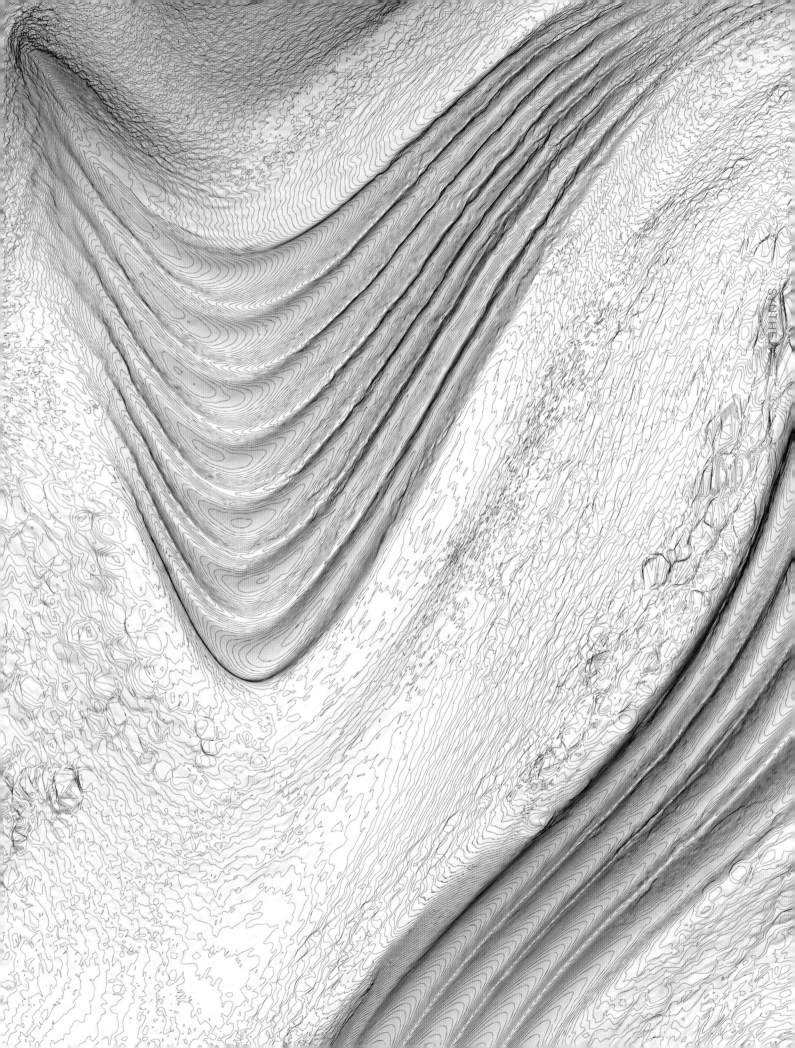

MANUFACTURED

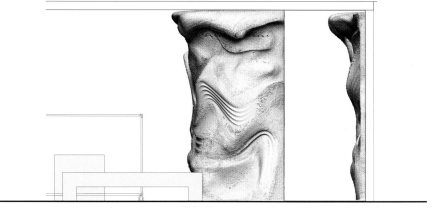

SIDE ELEVATION

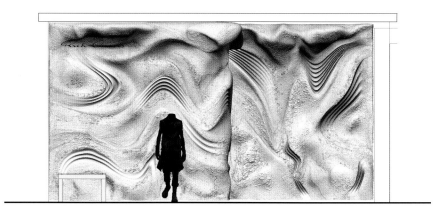

FRONT ELEVATION

ELEVATIONS

MANUFACTURED

WINDOW DISPLAY ON OXFORD STREET

Rick Owens

SYNTHETIC

INTO THE WOODS

WOODROW WILSON

NATURAL

LOS ANGELES, CALIFORNIA

STATUS: IN DEVELOPMENT
SITE: 18,000 SQ.FT.
AREA: 3,500 SQ.FT.
TYPE: RESIDENTIAL
PROGRAM: SINGLE FAMILY
DWELLING
OWNER: PRIVATE

The residence is to be built within a heavily wooded site in the Hollywood Hills. The secluded lot is located in the eclectic neighborhood of Runyon Canyon, minutes from Hollywood.

The strata of the hillside site translates into a layering of building strategies used to create the 3,500-square-foot house. A concrete base is burrowed into the hillside where the heavy foundation is expressed as simple concrete mass. The main living level opens to the gardens and to the views. The façade of glass allows for optimal transparency and is protected with a layer of screens that allow for sun protection and privacy. A faceted volume comprises the top level and contains the private functions of the home.

The floating mass is shaped by the constraints of the site and a series of openings that frame specific views.

The home is environmentally sound. Sustainable strategies include photovoltaics for power, a solar hydronic system for the heating of water and the latest in green technologies, materials and building systems. The distinct form of the building optimizes airflow, natural light and sun protection. The landscape is in keeping with the native flora. Drought-tolerant, native species compliment the existing palette of mature pines, eucalyptus and indigenous plants. A swimmers' pool creates a strong axis in the landscape. The windows of the pool open to the underground music studio.

NATURAL

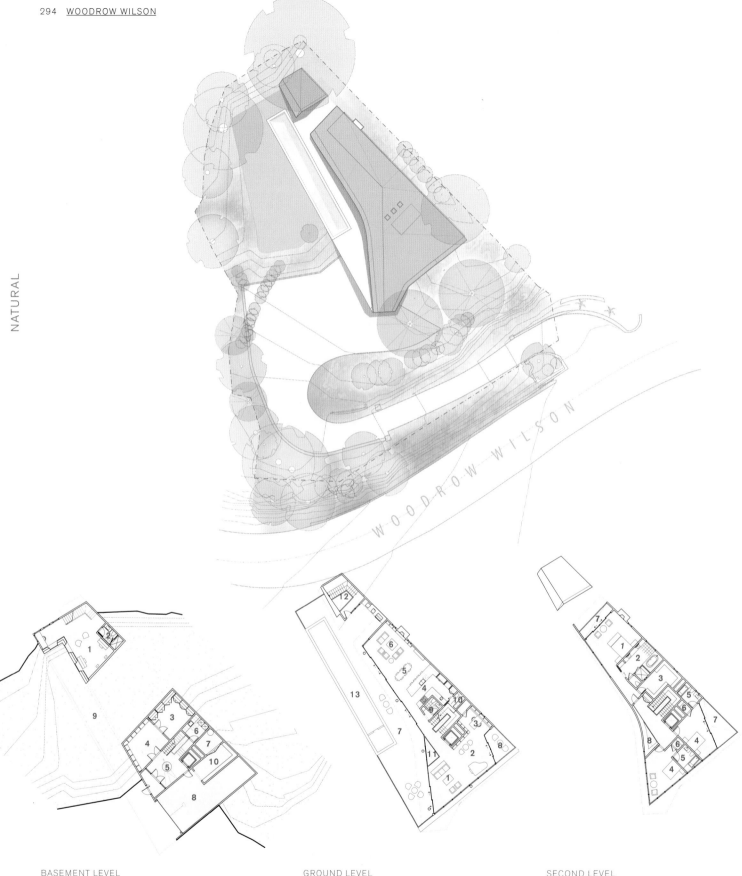

BASEMENT LEVEL
1. STUDIO 2. BATHROOM 3. GYM 4. MEDIA ROOM
5. ENTRY FOYER 6. LAUNDRY ROOM 7. MECHANICAL
ROOM 8. GARAGE 9. POOL 10. STORAGE

GROUND LEVEL
1. LIVING ROOM 2. LIBRARY 3. OFFICE
4. KITCHEN 5. DINING ROOM 6. FAMILY ROOM
7. DECK 8. BALCONY 9. POWDER ROOM
10. CLOSET 11. ATRIUM 12. STUDIO BELOW
13. POOL

SECOND LEVEL
1. MASTER BEDROOM 2. MASTER BATHROOM
3. MASTER CLOSET 4. BEDROOM 5. BATHROOM
6. CLOSET 7. BALCONY 8. ATRIUM

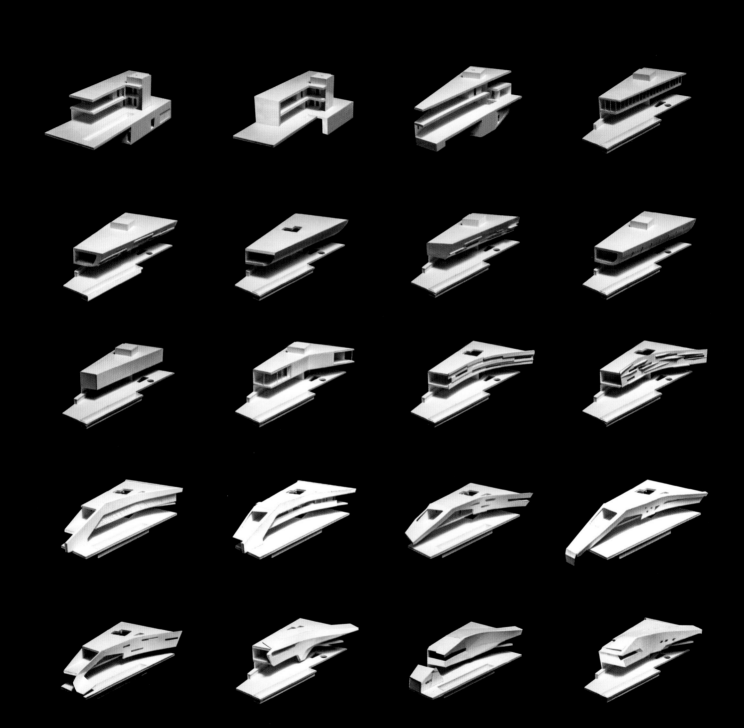

NATURAL

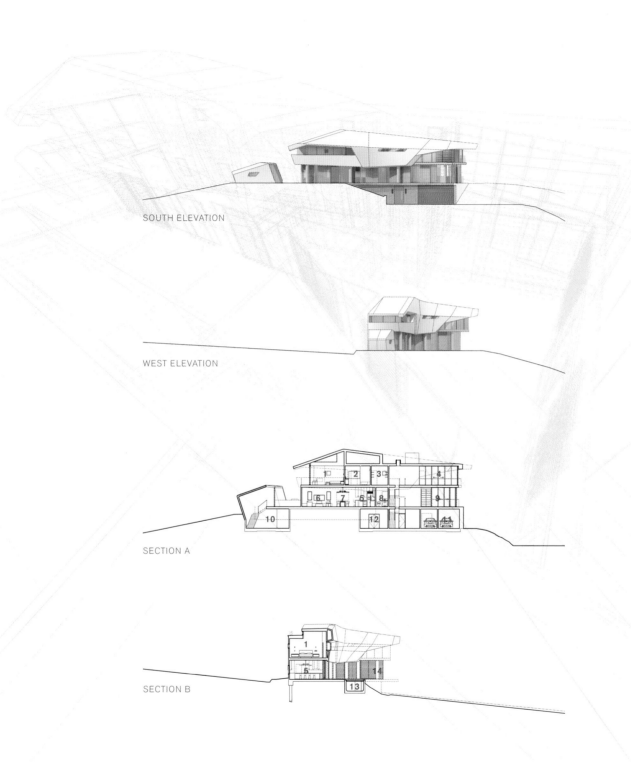

SOUTH ELEVATION

WEST ELEVATION

SECTION A

SECTION B

1. MASTER BEDROOM **2.** MASTER BATHROOM **3.** MASTER CLOSET **4.** BEDROOM **5.** KITCHEN
6. FAMILY ROOM **7.** DINING ROOM **8.** POWDER ROOM **9.** LIBRARY **10.** STUDIO **11.** GARAGE
12. STORAGE **13.** POOL **14.** DECK

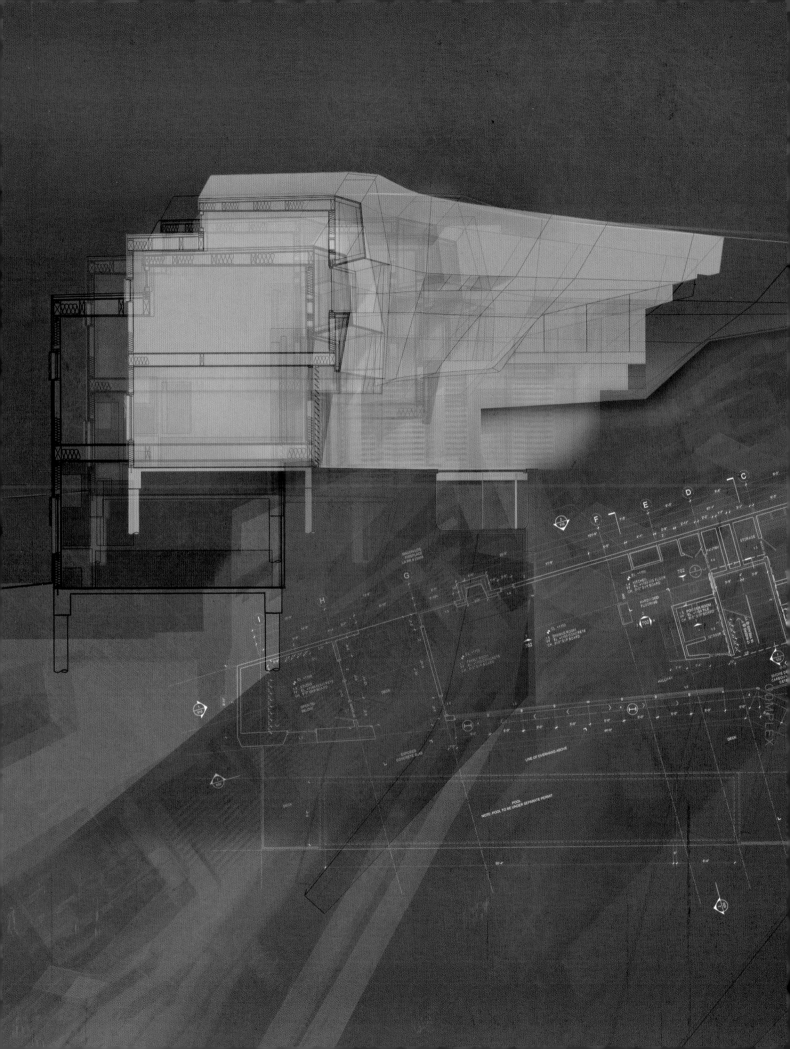

CORNERED

LA BREA HOUSING

WEST HOLLYWOOD,
CALIFORNIA

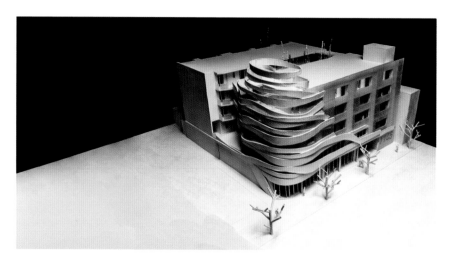

ACTUAL

STATUS: BUILT 2014
SITE: 14,000 SQ.FT.
AREA: 40,000 SQ.FT.
TYPE: MIXED USE
PROGRAM: 32 APARTMENTS,
COMMERCIAL SPACE
OWNER: WEST HOLLYWOOD
COMMUNITY HOUSING
CORP

The La Brea mixed-use affordable housing project for people living with disabilities is a 40,000-square-foot building for the city of West Hollywood. The design maximizes density, yet allocates ample outdoor space for residents. The site's 32 apartments are arranged around a shared exterior courtyard, parking is provided at grade, and the commercial space faces La Brea Avenue.

By nature, an affordable housing project is based on a simple, rational scheme. In this project, the design of the southwest corner stands in stark contrast to the rest of the project. It is more expressive and more sophisticated architecturally—a counterpoint to the rational order of the affordable housing project, built with sophisticated robotic fabrication techniques and digital design. In effect, it is a fifth elevation, highly visible from Santa Monica Boulevard and La Brea Avenue. It serves as the entry, containing social spaces, gardens, and circulation—a beacon of activity, with shared amenities.

The project was built for the city via a nonprofit developer that addresses the affordable housing shortage for tenants living with disabilities. The mixed-use program brings higher density to the urban core. The location within the central urban fabric ensures that residents have direct access to local businesses and services. Multiple public transportation options are directly accessible on the busy transit corridor of Santa Monica Boulevard, minimizing the need for private transportation.

The building exceeds the requirements of the Green Building Ordinance, emphasizing the commitment to environmental responsibility, green building, and sustainability. An outdoor courtyard features a garden accessible from all units. Each apartment has its own 80-square-foot private outdoor space with a designated storage room. Common areas are provided for the residents and for public use. Laundry facilities and other support spaces are included in the project.

ACTUAL

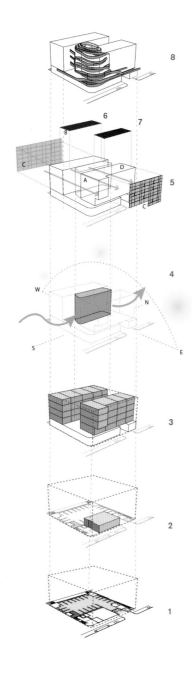

1. GROUND LEVEL PARKING 2. COMMERCIAL / RETAIL 3. 32 RESIDENTIAL UNITS 4. VERTICAL ATRIUM GARDEN 5. SCREENING FOR SUN PROTECTION, RAILING, AND PRIVACY 6. SOLAR HOT WATER 7. PHOTOVOLTAIC PANELS 8. STACKED GARDEN ATRIUM

ACTUAL

FIFTH LEVEL

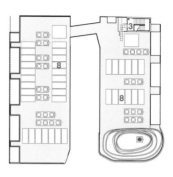

ROOF

THIRD LEVEL

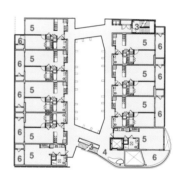

FOURTH LEVEL

A

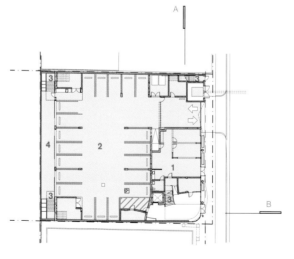

GROUND LEVEL

B

SECOND LEVEL

1. COMMERCIAL OFFICE **2.** PARKING **3.** CIRCULATION **4.** COMMON OPEN SPACE **5.** RESIDENTIAL
UNITS **6.** PRIVATE BALCONY SPACE **7.** COMMUNITY ROOM **8.** MECHANICAL ROOM

ACTUAL

EAST ELEVATION

SOUTH ELEVATION

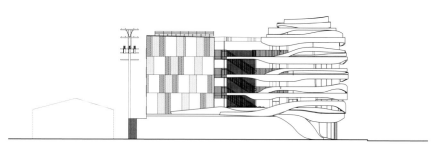

WEST ELEVATION

NORTH ELEVATION

ELEVATIONS

ACTUAL

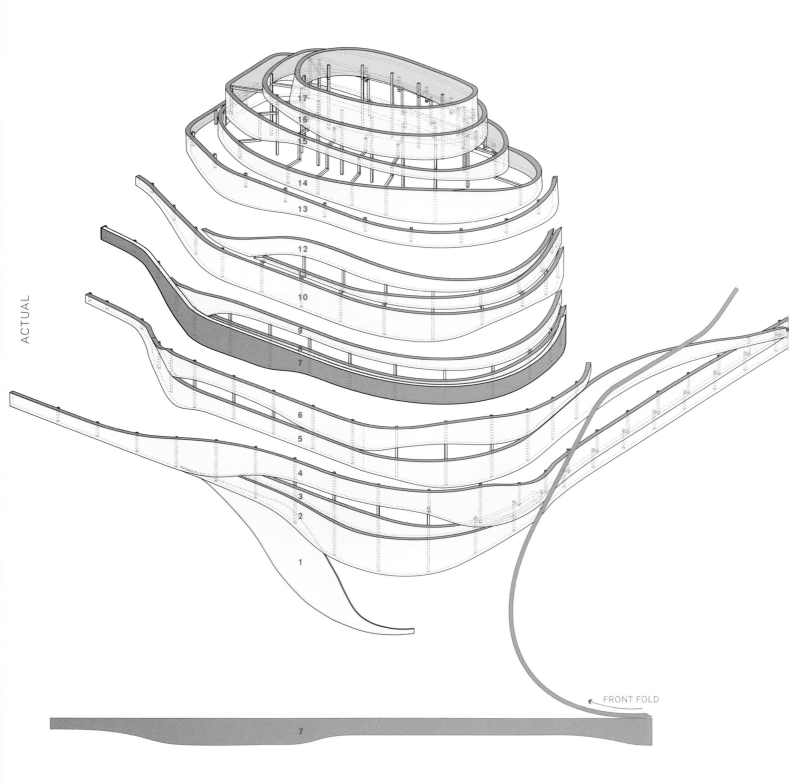

17

16

15

14

13

12

11

10

9

8

7

6

5

4

3

2

1

FRONT FOLD

7

BUILDING FAÇADE AXONOMETRIC

ACTUAL

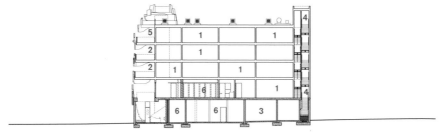

SECTION A

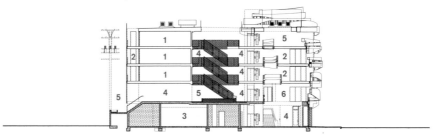

SECTION B

1. RESIDENTIAL **2.** PRIVATE OPEN SPACE **3.** PARKING **4.** CIRCULATION / UTILITY **5.** COMMON OPEN SPACE **6.** RETAIL / OFFICE / COMMUNITY ROOM

SECTIONS

ACTUAL

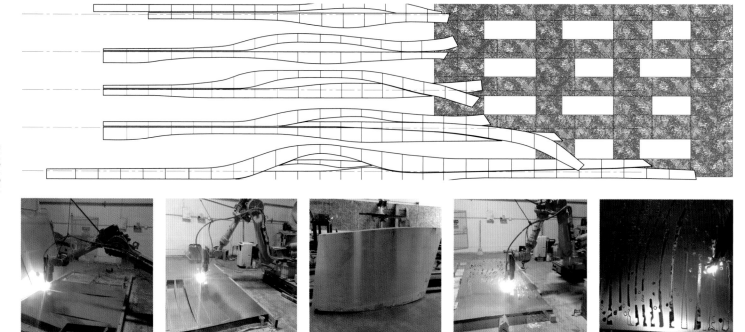

ACTUAL

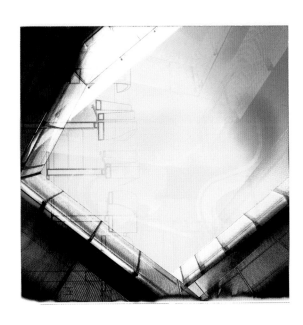

GUGGENHEIM HELSINKI

HELSINKI, FINLAND

ACTUAL

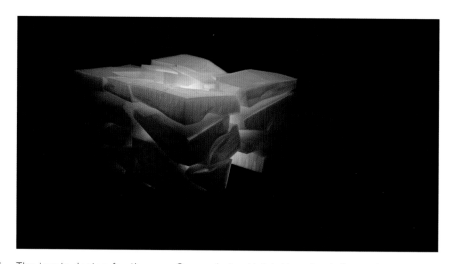

STATUS: COMPETITION 2014
SITE: 200,000 SQ.FT.
AREA: 130,000 SQ.FT.
TYPE: MUSEUM
PROGRAM: GALLERY,
GARDEN. EXHIBITION
SPACES, RESTAURANT.
BOOKSTORES
OWNER: SOLOMON R.
GUGGENHEIM FOUNDATION

The iconic design for the new Guggenheim, Helsinki, set on the waterfront, is a study in counterpoints—Finnish tradition and Helsinki's progressive mindset, traditional materials, and new technologies. Difference is also explored in the design of the three architectural components: the Grand Hall, a cluster of galleries; the Black Box, containing the public functions; the Spine Gallery, the conduit that unifies the elements and distinguishes the public from private areas. The design acts as a filter, investigating qualities of openness and porosity that permeate the complex; visual access to, from, and through the site; the scale, proportion, and placement of the building components in relation to neighboring buildings.

The northern portion of the site serves as a public plaza, an inviting social space that draws people from the city center. The Grand Hall contains galleries to house art with greater volume. Interstitial spaces allow natural light to filter through the mass into the common areas, while framing exterior views. A central circulation spire moves up through the mass, creating an open five-story void within the clusters of volumes. Reconfigurable spaces afford optimum flexibility to accommodate exhibition space, educational programs, lectures, special events, plus space to foster groundbreaking works. The horizontal gallery serves as a grand foyer into the main museum and adjacent sculpture garden courtyard. The omnipresent water and greenery are essential to the design. The Spine Gallery's public roof garden functions as a connective tissue between the public plaza to the north and the park Tähtitornin vuori to the south.

Contrasts, such as investigations of volume and mass versus openness and porosity, reference Finnish modernism in opposition to a future architectural vision. Similarly, raw materials, like concrete and heavy timber, are used in tandem with advanced material applications and fabrication methods, heightening the affect for visitors.

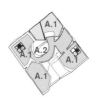

FIFTH LEVEL
A.1 EXHIBITION GALLERIES **A.2** SPIRAL GALLERY

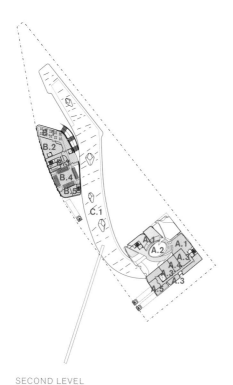

SECOND LEVEL
A.1 EXHIBITION GALLERIES **A.2** SPIRAL GALLERY **A.3** OFFICES
A.4 CONFERENCE ROOMS **A.5** STORAGE **B.1** RESTAURANT
B.2 KITCHEN **B.3** OFFICES **B.4** FLEXIBLE PERFORMANCE
B.5 GREEN ROOM **C.1** GARDEN

FOURTH LEVEL
A.1 EXHIBITION GALLERIES **A.2** SPIRAL GALLERY

ACTUAL

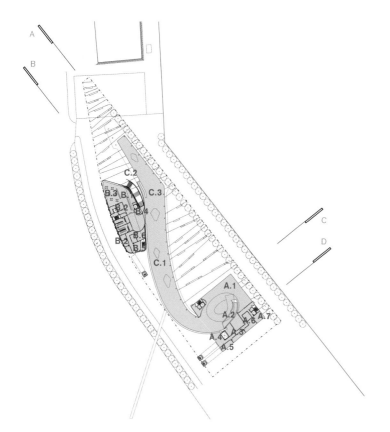

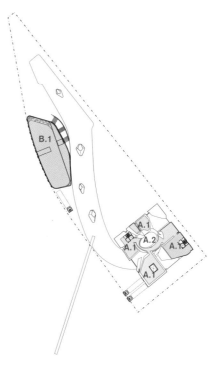

GROUND LEVEL
A.1 EXHIBITION GALLERIES **A.2** SPIRAL GALLERY **A.3** STORAGE
A.4 SHIPPING **A.5** STAGING **A.6** OFFICES **A.7** MULTIFUNCTION
CLASSROOM **B.1** MUSEUM AND DESIGN STORE **B.2** OFFICES
B.3 CAFÉ / BAR **B.4** COAT CHECK **B.5** STORAGE **B.6** STAFF LUNCH
ROOM **C.1** GALLERY **C.2** BAG CHECK **C.3** TICKETING

THIRD LEVEL
A.1 EXHIBITION GALLERIES **A.2** SPIRAL GALLERY
B.1 OUTDOOR RESTAURANT

FLOOR PLANS

ACTUAL

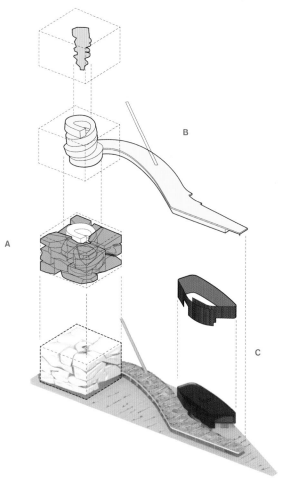

A. GRAND HALL

PACKED CLUSTER OF GALLERY VOLUMES • 14 GALLERIES THAT CAN BE USED INDIVIDUALLY OR WITH OTHERS • OPTIMAL FLEXIBILITY AND A VARIETY OF SPACES OFFERED • SPIRAL GALLERY / CIRCULATION IS CENTRAL TO MUSEUM • ATRIUM IS A 5-STORY GALLERY SPACE

B. SPINE GALLERY

CONNECTOR BETWEEN THE GRAND HALL AND THE BLACK BOX • LARGE HORIZONTAL GALLERY SPACE REMINISCENT OF BILBAO'S BOAT GALLERY • GALLERY ALSO SERVES AS CIRCULATION (INSIDE AND OUT) • THRESHOLD IS PROVIDED, IN ANTICIPATION OF ENTRY INTO THE GRAND HALL • VEGETATIVE ROOF IS A PUBLIC GREEN SPACE • THE ROOF IS AN EXTENSION OF THE PARK, CONNECTING THE PARK TO THE NORTH PLAZA

C. BLACK BOX

CONTAINS PUBLIC FUNCTIONS • OPENS TO THE CITY AND TO THE HARBOR • GRAND, HONORIFIC STAIR EXTENDS PUBLIC PLAZA • TRANSPARENT AND OPAQUE • BUILT-IN SCANDANAVIAN TRADI-TION WITH VERTICAL TIMBER, DARK TAR STAIN • GROUND FLOOR HOUSES CAFÉ, BOOKSTORE, MUSEUM SUPPORT SPACES • SECOND FLOOR CONTAINS RESTAURANT, BLACK BOX THEATER, KITCHEN

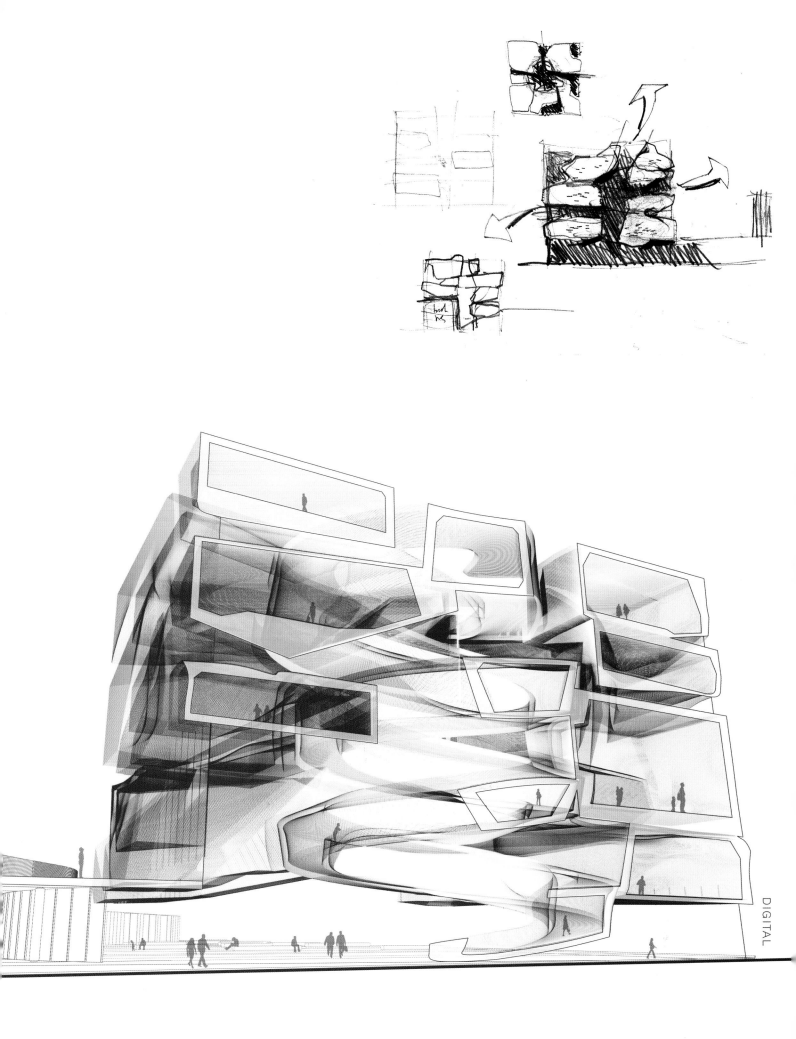

ACTUAL

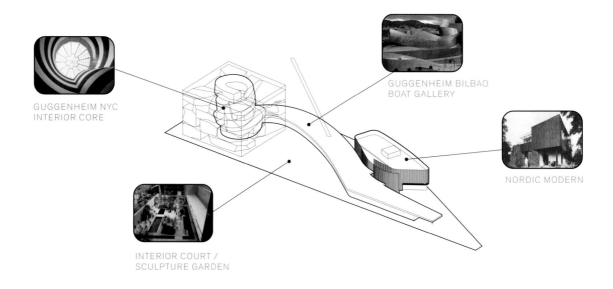

GUGGENHEIM NYC
INTERIOR CORE

GUGGENHEIM BILBAO
BOAT GALLERY

NORDIC MODERN

INTERIOR COURT /
SCULPTURE GARDEN

PRECEDENT DIAGRAM / ELEVATION

ACTUAL

ACKNOWLEDGEMENTS

I am fortunate to be surrounded by many talented people who continually challenge, stimulate, and inspire me. I am particularly indebted to the following for making the work possible. First of all, our consultants, tradespeople, artists, contractors and fabricators, especially Tom Farrage and Andreas Froesch, have all contributed to realizing our designs above and beyond our expectations. Art Gray's photographs, contained in this book, show our projects at their best. Many friends and colleagues offered assistance at various stages, in particular, Linda Hart. I owe a debt of gratitude to all the people in the office who have worked tirelessly over the years, notably Evelina Sausina, Yosuke Hoshina, and Risa Tsutsumi and most recently Kervin Lau, Mike Ho and Antonio Follo. I thank my colleagues at SCI-Arc for their support and encouragement, especially Eric Owen Moss; my colleagues at the USC School of Architecture, and those at the UCLA School of Architecture and Urban Design where I studied and remain connected. I would like to express my sincere appreciation to the many clients who have entrusted me with their projects. Among them, Dr. Harvey Karp, Nina Montee, Daniel Loeb, Michael Collins, Technicolor, and Douglas Elliman are deserving of special attention. Our developer clients and non-profit clients, including the West Hollywood Community Housing Corp., allow us the opportunity to design buildings that go the extra mile to help others. The generous fellowships I received from the American Academy in Rome and the MacDowell Colony provided me with the resources and opportunities to explore my ideas in nurturing, creative environments. To my colleagues and peers with whom I confer regularly—thank you for the support and friendly competition. Thanks to Thom Mayne who has been both mentor and friend for the past 20 years, generous with his advice, criticism, and encouragement. Finally, I am most appreciative of my partner in life, Tish, whose support and belief in the work (and me) from the very beginning have been unflagging and invaluable.

Thank you.......

COLLABORATORS

Michael Ho	Danny Xu	Zachery Main
Antonio Follo	David Hui	Michael Piscitello
Kervin Lau	Sean Oh	Yosuke Hoshina
Haleh Olfati	John Dalit	Risa Tsutsumi
Albert Chavez	William Hu	Kyd Kitchaiya
Bran Arifin	Nelson Almenderez	Mike Nesbit
Louie Bofill	Ted Digiralomo	Emmy Murata
Mina Jun	Oleg Korchinski	Peter Welch
Eric Giragosian	Gelareh Arbab	Phillip Rameriz
Joanne Kim	Hazel Aquino	Rene Freed
Katarina Ritcher	Grant Nunnelee	Peter Storey
Andreina Pepe	Barkev Damron	Jarod Poenisch
Shaler Campbell	Gonzalo Padilla	Daniel Innocente
Chia-Min Wang	Zachary Teixeria	Karla Mueller
Todd Swanson	Ryan Wynn	Nick Hopson
Pierina Merino	Justin Roth	Joseph Dangaran
Chris Penfold	Andrew Hammer	Axel Hess
Juliana Cianfaglione	Paul Andrzejczak	Florian Metz
Evelina Sausina	Hector Compagna	Leah Luxembaech
Jasmine Park	Tim Do	Motoko
Monica Mader	Han LIn	Nirad Gupta
Oscar DeLeon	Chis Mojo	Rene Tribble
James Choe	Lisa Little	David Orkand
Hemila Aria	Danny Chan	Jeff Buck
Joseph Lee	Wei Chei	Mike Yee
Pepe Sanchez	Cristin Dawson	Diana Oceguera
Chi Hang Lo	Wilson Ching	Jason Yaeger

AWARDS + PUBLICATIONS

INTERNATIONAL AND NATIONAL AWARDS

2015 **50 UNDER 50 AWARD**
Innovators of the 21st Century
Images Publishing Group, Australia

2015 **APA AWARD**
American Planning Association
La Brea Housing

2015 **BEST OF DESIGN AWARD**
Architect's Newspaper
Montee Karp Residence

2014 **NATIONAL AIA AWARD / HUD
SECRETARY'S HOUSING AWARD**
Sierra Bonita Mixed-Use
Affordable Housing

2014 **BEST OF YEAR AWARD**
Interior Design Magazine
Montee Karp Residence

2014 **BEST OF YEAR AWARD**
Interior Design Magazine
La Brea Affordable Housing

2014 **WORLD ARCHITECTURE /
INSIDE AWARD** (Shortlisted)
World Architecture Festival, Singapore
Montee Karp Residence

2013 **IDEAS AWARD FOR
EXCELLENCE IN STEEL FRAME
BUILDING DESIGN, AISC**
Sierra Bonita Affordable Housing

2012 **AMERICAN ARCHITECTURE
AWARD**
West Hollywood Housing

2012 **NATIONAL AIA AWARD / HONOR
AWARD FOR INTERIOR
ARCHITECTURE**
Out of Memory

2012 **ELEANOR BATEMAN SCHOLAR**
University of Massachusetts

2012 **SOCIAL ECONOMIC ENVIRONMENTAL
DESIGN AWARD FOR EXCELLENCE IN
PUBLIC INTEREST DESIGN** (SEED)
West Hollywood Housing

2011 **AMERICAN ARCHITECTURE
AWARD**
Out of Memory

2011 **ELEVATED TO COLLEGE OF
FELLOWS, AIA**

2011 **NATIONAL AIA AWARD HONOR
AWARD FOR INTERIOR
ARCHITECTURE**
Moving Picture Company

2011 **BEST OF YEAR AWARD**
Interior Design Magazine
Out of Memory

2011 **AWARD OF MERIT IN HOUSING AND
COMMUNITY DEVELOPMENT**
National Association of Housing and
Redevelopment Officials (NAHRO)
West Hollywood Housing

2011 **RESIDENTIAL ARCHITECT
DESIGN AWARD**
Residential Architect
West Hollywood Housing

2010 **BEST OF YEAR AWARD**
Interior Design Magazine
West Hollywood Housing

2009 **BEST OF YEAR AWARD**
Interior Design Magazine
Moving Picture Company

2009 **MACDOWELL COLONY
FELLOWSHIP**
Artist in Residency

2008 **PROGRESSIVE
ARCHITECTURE
AWARD (P/A AWARD)**
Nodul(ar) House

2007 **ROME PRIZE,
AMERICAN ACADEMY IN ROME**
Mercedes T. Bass Fellowship in
Architecture
Artist in Residency

2006 **NATIONAL AIA AWARD /
YOUNG ARCHITECT AWARD**
Patrick Tighe

2006 **BEST OF YEAR AWARD**
Interior Design Magazine
LA Loft

2006 **40 UNDER 40 AWARD**
Building Design and
Construction Magazine
Patrick Tighe

2006 **NATIONAL AIA AWARD /
SMALL PROJECT AWARD**
Storefront

2005 **NATIONAL AIA AWARD /
SMALL PROJECT AWARD**
Black Box

2004 **AMERICAN ARCHITECTURE AWARD**
The Chicago Athenaeum
Live Oak Studio

2003 **AMERICAN ARCHITECTURE AWARD**
The Chicago Athenaeum
Collins Gallery

2003 **HOUSE OF THE MONTH AWARD** (June)
Architectural Record Magazine
Collins Gallery

2003 **NATIONAL AIA AWARD / HONOR
AWARD FOR INTERIOR ARCHITECTURE**
Collins Gallery

2001 **NATIONAL AIA AWARD / HONOR
AWARD FOR INTERIOR ARCHITECTURE**
Jacobs Subterranean

REGIONAL AWARDS

2015 **AIACC DESIGN HONOR AWARD**
California Chapter of the AIA
Montee Karp Residence

2015 **AIA SOUTH BAY DESIGN AWARD**
South Bay Chapter of the AIA
Garrison Residence

2015 **CALIFORNIA HOME + DESIGN AWARD**
California Home + Design Magazine
Montee Karp Residence

2013 **CALIFORNIA AIA AWARD / HONOR
AWARD FOR ARCHITECTURE**
West Hollywood Housing

2012 **WESTSIDE PRIZE**
Westside Urban Forum
La Brea Affordable Housing

2011 **AWARD OF EXCELLENCE IN
SUSTAINABLE DEVELOPMENT**
CRA (California Redevelopment
Association) West Hollywood Housing

2011 **AWARD OF MERIT FOR STRUCTURAL
ENGINEERING**
Structural Engineers Association of
Southern California (SEAOSC)
West Hollywood Housing

2011 **PLANNING IN EXCELLENCE IN
IMPLEMENTATION AWARD**
American Planning Association,
California Chapter
West Hollywood Housing

2011 **PLANNING IN EXCELLENCE IN
IMPLEMENTATION AWARD**
American Planning Association,
Los Angeles Chapter
West Hollywood Housing

2011 **WESTSIDE PRIZE**
Westside Urban Forum
Moving Picture Company

2010 **SCANPH AFFORDABLE HOUSING
AWARD** (Special Needs)
Southern California Association of
Non-Profit Housing
Sierra Bonita Affordable Housing

2010 **WESTSIDE PRIZE**
Westside Urban Forum
Sierra Bonita Affordable Housing

					2008	**A+D MUSEUM**
						Los Angeles, CA
						AIA Design Award Winners Exhibition

2009 **LOS ANGELES ARCHITECTURAL AWARD** Los Angeles Business Council Moving Picture Company

2015 **A+D MUSEUM**
Los Angeles, CA
Shelter: Rethinking how we live in LA

2008 **NEW YORK CENTER FOR ARCHITECTURE**
New York, NY
Progressive Architecture Award
Winners Exhibition

2008 **AIA LOS ANGELES DESIGN AWARD**
Honor Award for Architecture
Tigertail

2015 **UNIVERSITY OF SOUTHERN CALIFORNIA**
Los Angeles, CA
Waiting for Guggenheim Exhibition

2007 **UCLA, PERLOFF GALLERY**
Los Angeles, CA
Uncontested Exhibition

2008 **LOS ANGELES ARCHITECTURAL AWARD**
Los Angeles Business Council
Sierra Bonita Affordable Housing

2015 **AIA NATIONAL CONVENTION**
Chicago, IL
National Honor Awards Exhibition

2006 **A+D MUSEUM**
Los Angeles, CA
New Blood, Next Generation Exhibition

2006 **DISTINGUISHED SUSTAINABLE BUSINESS AWARD**
Greenopia

2013 **MUSEUM OF CONTEMPORARY ART (MOCA)** Los Angeles, CA
Contemporary Architecture from
Southern California

2006 **NEOCON/LA DESIGN WEEK**
Los Angeles, CA
LA Loft: 2026 Installation

2005 **FRESH ART COMPETITION WINNER**
City of Santa Monica, Commission for
Public Art Installation, Ocean Park Shell

2013 **A+D MUSEUM**
Los Angeles, CA
Never Built Los Angeles

2005 **HERMAN MILLER**
New York, NY
American Architecture Exhibition

2004 **AIA LOS ANGELES NEXT LA AWARD**
Norwalk Affordable Housing

2012 **BIG CITY FORUM EXHIBITION**
Los Angeles, CA
Maximum Change

2005 **HERMAN MILLER**
Los Angeles, CA
American Architecture Exhibition

2001 **AIA LOS ANGELES NEXT LA AWARD**
Live Oak Studio

2012 **JOE'S VENICE**
Los Angeles, CA
Artists X Architects

2005 **AUBURN UNIVERSITY**
Auburn, AL
Soft Boundaries Exhibition

INTERNATIONAL EXHIBITIONS

2012 **NEW YORK CENTER FOR ARCHITECTURE**
New York, NY
Change, Contemporary Architecture
in the Middle East 2000–present

2005 **CLOVER PARK**
Santa Monica, CA
Fresh Art, A Public Art Installation

2015 **INTERNATIONAL CONFERENCE**
Istanbul, Turkey
Computer Aided Design in
Architecture Exhibition

2014 **INTERNATIONAL CONFERENCE**
Istanbul, Turkey
Computer Aided Design in
Architecture Exhibition

2012 **AIA NATIONAL CONVENTION**
Washington DC
National Honor Awards Exhibition

2005 **CHICAGO ATHENAEUM: MUSEUM OF ARCHITECTURE AND DESIGN**
Chicago, IL
American Architecture Exhibition

2012 **ISTANBUL BIENNALE**
Istanbul, Turkey
The City and the World Exhibition

2011 **UCLA, PERLOFF GALLERY**
Los Angeles, CA
Distinguished Alumni Exhibition

2005 **AIA NATIONAL CONVENTION**
Las Vegas, NV
National Honor Awards Exhibition

2011 **INTERNATIONAL BIENNALE OF ARCHITECTURE**
Buenos Aires, Argentina
New World Architecture Exhibition

2011 **AIA NATIONAL CONVENTION**
New Orleans, LA
National Honor Awards Exhibition

2005 **A+D MUSEUM**
Los Angeles, CA
Communities Under Construction
Exhibition, City Works Los Angeles

2011 **PRAGUE QUADRENNIAL**
Prague, Czech Republic
US Architecture Exhibition

2011 **SCI-ARC GALLERY**
Los Angeles, CA
Out of Memory

2005 **UCLA, PERLOFF GALLERY**
Los Angeles, CA
Past Present Future Exhibition

2007 **AMERICAN ACADEMY IN ROME**
Rome, Italy
Fellows Exhibition

2010 **DESIGN TRUST FOR PUBLIC SPACE**
New York, NY
Benefit Exhibition

2004 **CHICAGO ATHENAEUM: MUSEUM OF ARCHITECTURE AND DESIGN**
Chicago, IL
New American Architecture Exhibition

2007 **BIAGIOTTI GALLERY**
Florence, Italy
Stars and Stripes, Group Show

2010 **UCLA, PERLOFF GALLERY**
Los Angeles, CA
Past Present Future Exhibition

2004 **HENNESSEY + INGALLS**
Santa Monica, CA
"Brave New Houses" Exhibition

NATIONAL EXHIBITIONS

2010 **WOODBURY GALLERY**
Hollywood, CA
Fast, Cheap & Out of Control Exhibition

2015 **NEW YORK CENTER FOR ARCHITECTURE**
New York, NY
Designing Affordability:
Quicker, Smarter, More Efficient
Housing Now.

2009 **UCLA, PERLOFF GALLERY**
Los Angeles, CA
Distinguished Alumni Exhibition

2004 **AIA HEADQUARTERS**
Washington DC
AIA Honors Awards Exhibition

2004	**AIA NATIONAL CONVENTION** San Diego, CA National Honor Awards Exhibition	2010	**WORKPLACE DESIGN** by Helen Parton Thames and Hudson, London, England Moving Picture Company	2008	**THE PHAIDON ATLAS OF 21ST CENTURY WORLD ARCHITECTURE** Phaidon Press Ltd, London, England Live Oak Studio
2001	**AIA NATIONAL CONVENTION** Denver, CO National Honor Awards Exhibition	2010	**ARCHITECTURE ZONE A TO Z** Rihan CC, Shanghai, China Tigertail	2008	**SIGNIFICANT INTERIORS, AIA** Images Publishing, Melbourne, Australia Jacobs Subterranean, Collins Gallery

BOOKS

2015	**FIFTY UNDER FIFTY** Images Publishing, Melbourne, Australia Profile, Patrick Tighe Architecture by Beverly Russell, Eva L. Maddox & Farooq Ameen	2010	**COLLECTION: OFFICES** by Chris Van Uffelen Verlagshaus Braun, Switzerland Moving Picture Company	2007	**YOUNG ARCHITECTS AMERICAS** Daab Publishers, Cologne, Germany LA Loft, Collins Gallery, Trahan Ranch
2013	**A NEW SCULPTURALISM: CONTEMPORARY ARCHITECTURE** from Southern California, MOCA Rizzoli, New York, NY	2010	**ARCHITECTURE X FILE 100 IDEAS** Rihan CC, Shanghai, China Sierra Bonita Mixed-Use Affordable Housing, Nodul(ar) House	2007	**100 GREAT EXTENSIONS AND RENOVATIONS** by Philip Jodidio Images Publishing, Melbourne, Australia Black Box, Live Oak Studio, Ashcroft Studio, Jacobs Subterranean,
2012	**BEST OF YEAR ARCHITECTURE & DESIGN 2011** Sandow Media, New York, NY West Hollywood Housing	2010	**IN HOME** Rihan CC, Shanghai, China LA Loft	2007	**CONVERSIONS** by Emma O'Kelly & Corinna Dean Laurence King Publishing, London, England LA Loft
2011	**200 HOUSES** by Mark Cleary Images Publishing, Melbourne, Australia Tigertail	2009	**LIVING WEST** by Sam Lubell Monacelli Press, New York, NY Tigertail	2007	**MODERN CABIN** by Michelle Kodis Gibbs Smith Publishing, Salt Lake City, UT Black Box
2011	**WORKING SPACES TODAY** Links Books, Barcelona, Spain Moving Picture Company	2009	**ARCHITECTURE AND DESIGN LOS ANGELES** Fusion Publishing, Berlin, Germany LA Loft	2007	**THE DESIGN STUDIO: DEVELOPING TECHNICAL AND CREATIVE SKILLS** by Carolyn Gibbs Fairchild Books, New York, NY Trahan Ranch
2011	**TOTAL OFFICE DESIGN: 50 CONTEMPORARY WORK PLACES** by Helen Parton Thames and Hudson, London, England Moving Picture Company	2009	**COLLECTION: US ARCHITECTURE** by Michelle Galindo Verlagshaus Braun, Switzerland Tigertail	2007	**MICRO ARCHITECTURE** by Ruth Slavid Laurence King Publishing, London, England OP Shell
2011	**TOP SPACE 2** Artpower, Beijing, China Moving Picture Company	2009	**PUBLIC SPACE** Rihan CC, Shanghai, China Moving Picture Company	2007	**INDEX** Journal of the American Academy in Rome AAR Publications, Rome, Italy
2010	**2010 WORLD INTERIOR DESIGN IMAGE** Saihan Cultural, Shanghai, China Moving Picture Company	2009	**DETAILS IN ARCHITECTURE: CREATIVE DETAILING BY LEADING ARCHITECTS** by Andrew Hall Images Publishing, Melbourne, Australia Moving Picture Company	2006	**2000 ARCHITECTS** by Aisha Hasanovic Images Publishing, Melbourne, Australia Trahan Ranch, Collins Gallery, Jacobs Subterranean, Live Oak Studio, Ashcroft Studio
2010	**BEST SELECTION OF SHANGLIN** Designer Books, Shanglin, China LA Loft, Sierra Bonita Mixed-Use Affordable Housing, Tigertail	2009	**100 COUNTRY HOUSES, NEW RURAL ARCHITECTURE** by Beth Browne Images Publishing, Melbourne, Australia Trahan Ranch	2006	**A POCKETFUL OF HOUSES** by Robyn Beaver Images Publishing, Melbourne, Australia Trahan Ranch
2010	**THE POWER OF PRO BONO** by John Cary Metropolis Books, New York, NY Sierra Bonita Mixed-Use Affordable Housing	2009	**HOLLYWOOD BACHELOR PADS** by Carol Kipling Schiffer, New York, NY Collins Gallery	2006	**IDEAS FOR GREAT KITCHENS** Sunset Books, Menlo Park, CA Collins Gallery
2010	**A5 LA** by Charles Casey Matthewson Oro Publishing, San Francisco, CA Tigertail, Sierra Bonita Mixed-Use Affordable Housing, Moving Picture Company, Villa Skhirat	2008	**1000X ARCHITECTURE OF THE AMERICAS** Verlagshaus Braun, Switzerland Tigertail, LA Loft	2005	**100 MORE OF THE WORLD'S BEST HOUSES** by Michelle Galindo Images Publishing, Melbourne, Australia Trahan Ranch
		2008	**COLLECTION: HOUSES** by Michelle Galindo Verlagshaus Braun, Switzerland Tigertail		

2005   **OPENINGS**
by Wendy Talerico
Wiley, New York, NY
Collins Gallery

2005   **HOUSE PLUS**
by Phyllis Richardson
Thames and Hudson, London, England
Live Oak Studio

2005   **SMALL CITY HOUSES**
Loft Publications, Barcelona, Spain
Black Box Studio

2004   **THE NEW AMERICAN DREAM**
by James Gauer
Monacelli, New York, NY
Collins Gallery

2004   **1000 ARCHITECTS**
Images Publishing, Melbourne, Australia
Trahan Ranch, Jacobs Subterranean,
Collins Gallery

2004   **HOLLYWOOD STYLE**
by Diane Dorran Saeks
Rizzoli, New York, NY
Live Oak Studio

2004   **LOS ANGELES ARCHITECTURE
AND DESIGN**
by Karen Mahle
teNeues Publishing, New York, NY
Collins Gallery

2003   **BRAVE NEW HOUSES, ADVENTURES
IN SOUTHERN CALIFORNIA LIVING**
by Michael Webb (cover)
Rizzoli, New York, NY
Collins Gallery

INTERNATIONAL PUBLICATIONS

2015   **DETAILS** (Korea)
Issue 34
La Brea Housing

2015   **GA HOUSES** (Japan)
Issue 144
Trahan Ranch

2015   **WALLPAPER** (Italy)
Limited Edition Cover by Rick Owens
Rick Owens Showroom

2015   **GA HOUSES** (Japan)
Issue 140
Montee Karp Residence, Tigertail,
Trahan Ranch

2015   **ARCHITECTURE / DETAIL** (China)
Magazine
La Brea Housing

2015   **405 ARCHITECTURE + CULTURE**
(Korea)

2015   **FRAME** (Netherlands)
"Light Shadow" by Matthew Hurst
Rick Owens Showroom

2011   **FRAME** (Netherlands)
"White Noise" by Michael Webb
Out of Memory

2011   **AZURE** "The Common Good"
by Michael Webb
West Hollywood Housing

2008   **A+U** (Japan)
"Young LA Architects"
Nodul(ar) House, LA Loft,
Moving Picture Company

2010   **MEN'S VOGUE MAGAZINE** (Brazil)
"Innovative Designs"
Moving Picture Company

2010   **TIERRA EDICION 6** (Mexico) (cover)
"Ultra Modern"
Moving Picture Company, LA Loft,
Mar Vista House, Tigertail

2010   **ATTITUDE** (Portugal)
"The New Office"
Moving Picture Company

2010   **CASA & MERCADO MAGAZINE** (Brazil)
"Light and Shadow"
Moving Picture Company

2010   **VILLA JOURNAL** (Czech Republic)
"Geometry Systematically Ruled
by Chaos"
Mar Vista House

2010   **SWISS BUSINESS** (Switzerland)
"Immobilien & Business Verlags AG"
Moving Picture Company

2010   **SPA-DE VOL. 13** (Japan)
"Moving Picture Company"
Moving Picture Company

2010   **FRAME** (Netherlands)
"1DX"
Moving Picture Company

2010   **CEDAR WINGS, MIDDLE EAST
AIRLINES** (Lebanon)
"Thinking 'Outside the Cubicle':
World's Most Original Offices"
Moving Picture Company

2010   **HINGE VOL. 173** (Hong Kong)
"Office Life"
Moving Picture Company

2009   **COMPASSES** (United Arab Emirates)
"Southern California Experiments"
by Livio Sacchi
Moving Picture Company

2009   **ARCHITECTURE/TRENDS**
(Russia) (cover)
"LLC Forward Media Group"
Moving Picture Company

2009   **BOB 062** (Korea)
"Tighe Architecture Profile"
Tigertail, Sierra Bonita, Moving
Picture Company, Nodul(ar) House,
Mar Vista House
LA Loft

2009   **CAN** (China)
"Best Offices 2009"
Moving Picture Company

2009   **HOME JOURNAL** VOL. 30, NO. 348
(Hong Kong) "Infocus"
LA Loft

2009   **HOME JOURNAL** VOL. 29, NO. 347
(Hong Kong) "Infocus"
Moving Picture Company

2009   **FX** (UK)
"World Class Office Design"
Moving Picture Company

2009   **DETAILS** Issue 14 (Korea)
"California Architects"
Tigertail

2009   **OUT LOOK** (China)
"New Housing"
Sierra Bonita Mixed-Use
Affordable Housing

2009   **PANORAMA** (Spain)
"California Residences"
Mar Vista House

2009   **KAPITAL** (Norway)
"Moving Picture Company"
Moving Picture Company

2009   **SPADE** (Canada)
"Los Angeles Work Spaces"
Moving Picture Company

2006   **NOI THAT** (Vietnam)
"A Ranch in Texas"
by Ho Trung Chanh
Trahan Ranch

2006   **HINGE VOL. 135** (Hong Kong)
"Project File"
LA Loft

2006   **HINGE VOL. 128** (Hong Kong)
"Global Perspective"
Jacobs Subterranean, Collins Gallery,
Trahan Ranch, Ashcroft Residence,
Live Oak Studio

2005   **PEN NO.149** (Tokyo)
"Los Angeles Gallery"
Collins Gallery

2005   **MONUMENT VOL. 69** (Australia)
"Home on The Range"
by Elizabeth Martin
Trahan Ranch

2005	**KENCHIKU NOTE** (Japan) "United Project Files" by Seibundo Shinkasha Collins Gallery
2005	**DETAILS** ISSUE 5 (Korea) "Los Angeles Gallery" Collins Gallery
2002	**MONUMENT** VOL. 49 (Australia) "West Coast Aesthetic" by Elizabeth Martin Collins Gallery

NATIONAL PUBLICATIONS

2015	**CALIFORNIA HOME + DESIGN** "The Perfect Pacific Perch" by Lindsey Shook
2015	**NEW YORK TIMES** "A Room with a View? Pick any you want" by Sarah Amelar Montee Karp Residence
2015	**INTERIOR DESIGN MAGAZINE** "Best of Year" Montee Karp Residence, La Brea Affordable Housing
2014	**INTERIOR DESIGN MAGAZINE** (cover) "From a Different Angle" by Edie Cohen Montee Karp Residence
2014	**WALLPAPER MAGAZINE** (cover) Rick Owens Showroom
2014	**WEST HOLLYWOOD MAGAZINE** (cover) "Patrick Tighe - Inserting Big Design into Small Spaces" by Gus Heulley Profile, Patrick Tighe Architecture
2014	**ARCHITECT MAGAZINE** "La Brea Housing" by Nate Berg La Brea Affordable Housing
2012	**METROPOLIS MAGAZINE** (cover) "Building on Shifting Sands" by John Hockenberry Villa Skhirat
2012	**ARCHITECT MAGAZINE** AIA National Awards Out of Memory
2012	**URBAN LAND,** (Magazine of the ULI) "Noteworthy US Affordable Housing Developments" by Ron Nyren West Hollywood Housing
2012	**ARCHITECT MAGAZINE** "Family Sized" by Elizabeth Evitts Dickinson West Hollywood Housing
2011	**INTERIOR DESIGN MAGAZINE** "Best of Year" by Annie Block Out of Memory

2011	**URBAN HOME, MODERN** (cover) "Rural Oasis" by Sharla Bell Trahan Ranch
2011	**THE ATLANTIC CITIES** "Affordable Housing That Doesn't Scream Affordable" by Allison Arieff West Hollywood Housing
2011	**CALIFORNIA HOME + DESIGN** 10 to Watch "The Equalizer" by Mary Jo Bowling and Lydia Lee Profile, Patrick Tighe
2011	**FORM** "Sierra Bonita Apartments" by Caren Kurlander Sierra Bonita Affordable Housing
2011	**ARCHITECT MAGAZINE** AIA National Awards Moving Picture Company
2011	**RESIDENTIAL ARCHITECT MAGAZINE** "Residential Architecture Awards" by Meghan Drueding West Hollywood Housing
2011	**arcCA** "Valuing the AIA: A Conversation Across Generations" by Gray Dougherty Profile, Patrick Tighe
2011	**INTERIOR DESIGN MAGAZINE** "Out of Memory" by Edie Cohen Out of Memory
2011	**ANGELENO** "Space Crafter" by Gary Baum Profile, Patrick Tighe
2010	**INTERIOR DESIGN MAGAZINE** "Best of Year" by Annie Block Sierra Bonita Mixed-Use Affordable Housing
2010	**INTERIOR DESIGN MAGAZINE** "West Hollywood Housing Project" by Eddie Cohen Sierra Bonita Affordable Housing
2010	**INTERIOR DESIGN MAGAZINE** "Only Imagine" by Edie Cohen Tigertail
2010	**INTERIORS & SOURCES** "Picture Show" Moving Picture Company
2009	**INTERIOR DESIGN** "Best of Year" by Annie Block Moving Picture Company
2009	**INTERIOR DESIGN** "Special Effects" by Edie Cohen Moving Picture Company

2009	**FORM** "Public Work" Sierra Bonita Mixed-Use Affordable Housing
2009	**USC ARCHITECTURE SCHOOL JOURNAL, IDNWS** Interview by Gail Borden Profile, Patrick Tighe
2008	**FORM** "Los Angeles AIA Design Awards" Tigertail
2008	**ARCHITECT MAGAZINE** (cover) "P/A Awards" by Katie Gerfen Nodul(ar) House
2007	**NEWSWEEK** "Small City, Big Impact How West Hollywood is Casting Itself as a Green Leader" by Andrew Murr Sierra Bonita Mixed-Use Affordable Housing
2007	**INTERIOR DESIGN** "Sustainability Issue" Eco-Lux on Melrose
2006	**INTERIOR DESIGN** "Best of Year" LA Loft
2006	**LA ARCHITECT** "Progress Report," Profile Tigertail, Sierra Bonita Mixed-Use Affordable Housing
2006	**BOULEVARD** "Futuristic Homes" by Brooke Kelly LA Loft
2006	**LA ARCHITECT** "Selling" Eco-Lux on Melrose
2006	**LA ARCHITECT** "2026 Fine Living" by Jennifer Caterino LA Loft
2006	**SOUTHERN CALIFORNIA HOME AND OUTDOOR** (cover) "The Future Is Now" by Dede Ginter LA Loft
2006	**INTERIOR DESIGN** (cover) "Future Shock" by Edie Cohen LA Loft
2006	**DESERT LIVING** "Installation: Fine Living 2026" LA Loft
2006	**RESIDENTIAL ARCHITECT** "Imagine and Create" by Meghan Drueding Live Oak Studio

2006	**BUILDING DESIGN AND CONSTRUCTION** **"40 UNDER 40"** Profile, Patrick Tighe
2006	**CALIFORNIA HOME AND DESIGN** "Central Themes" by Sally Schultheiss Trahan Ranch, LA Loft
2006	**LA INSIDE** (cover) "Living 2026 The Future of Live-Work and Design" LA Loft
2006	**INTERIOR DESIGN** "On The Half Shell" by Greg Goldin OP Shell
2005	**LA ARCHITECT** "Movement" Perth Amboy High School
2005	**LA ARCHITECT** "LA vs NY" Profile, Patrick Tighe Architecture
2005	**LA ARCHITECT** "LA AIA Design Awards" Norwalk Housing
2004	**ARCHITECTURAL DIGEST** "A Hill Country Harbinger" by Philip Nobel Trahan Ranch
2004	**ARCHITECTURAL RECORD** "Off the Beaten Path" by David Dillion Trahan Ranch
2004	**ANGELENO** "Home is Where The Art Is" by Matthew Giles Collins Gallery
2004	**DETAILS** "Square Roots" by Christopher Campbell Black Box
2004	**LA ARCHITECT** "Architecture and Art" by David Leroy Collins Gallery
2004	**SUNSET MAGAZINE** "L.A. Oasis" by Jill Peters Collins Gallery
2003	**INTERIOR DESIGN** "From Capri to California" by Edie Cohen Live Oak Studio
2003	**ARCHITECTURAL RECORD** "AIA National Honor Awards" Collins Gallery
2003	**ANGELENO** "Neighborhood Gems" by Jack Skelley Jacobs Subterranean

2002	**INTERIOR DESIGN** "For Your Eyes Only" by Cindy Allen Collins Gallery
2002	**ARCHITECTURAL DIGEST** "Up The Down Staircase" by Peter Halderman Jacobs Subterranean
2002	**INTERIOR DESIGN** "Art For Life" by Edie Cohen Collins Gallery
2002	**LA ARCHITECT** "LA AIA Design Awards" Live Oak Studio
2001	**LA ARCHITECT** (cover) "A Grand Small House" Collins Gallery
2001	**LA ARCHITECT** (cover) "Finding a Voice" Jacobs Subterranean
2001	**LA ARCHITECT** "Finding A Voice–Emerging Architects" by Elizabeth Martin Profile, Patrick Tighe Architecture
2001	**ARCHITECTURAL RECORD** "National AIA Honors" Jacobs Subterranean

NEWSPAPERS

2015	**THE ARCHITECT'S NEWSPAPER** 2015 Best of Design Awards Montee Karp Residence
2014	**THE ARCHITECT'S NEWSPAPER** 09 "Cornered" by Michael Webb La Brea Affordable Housing
2014	**THE NEW YORK TIMES** "Pick a View, Any View" by Sarah Amelar, Montee Karp Residence
2011	**LA WEEKLY** Best of LA People 2011 Profile, Patrick Tighe
2011	**THE ARCHITECT'S NEWSPAPER** 02 "Out of Memory" by Michael Webb Sci-Arc Installation
2010	**THE ARCHITECT'S NEWSPAPER** 10 "Crit" by Sam Lubell Sierra Bonita Mixed-Use Affordable Housing
2009	**THE ARCHITECT'S NEWSPAPER** 07 "Interiors" by Sam Lubell Moving Picture Company
2009	**THE ARCHITECT'S NEWSPAPER** 02 "Best In Show" by Sam Lubell Tigertail

2008	**THE ARCHITECT'S NEWSPAPER** 07 "Getting Dense" by Sam Lubell Sierra Bonita Affordable Housing
2008	**THE ARCHITECT'S NEWSPAPER** "P/A Awards," Nodul(ar) House
2006	**THE NEW YORK TIMES** "Young Architect Award Recipients" by Robin Pobegrin 2006 AIA Young Architects Award, Patrick Tighe
2004	**LOS ANGELES TIMES MAGAZINE** "Covering All the Angles" by Michael Webb Live Oak Studio
2004	**LOS ANGELES TIMES MAGAZINE** "California Dreaming" by Barbara Thornburg Skylark Lane
2003	**LOS ANGELES TIMES MAGAZINE** (cover) "Living With Art" by Barbara Thornburg Collins Gallery
2002	**LOS ANGELES TIMES MAGAZINE** "High Resolution" by Barbara Thornburg Collins Gallery

LECTURES

2016	**CALIFORNIA STATE POLYTECHNIC UNIVERSITY, POMONA** Pomona, CA "Building Dichotomy"
2015	**UNIVERSITY OF SOUTHERN CALIFORNIA** Los Angeles, CA "Waiting for Guggenheim" A panel discussion, Guggenheim Helsinki International Competition Entries
2014	**OTIS COLLEGE OF ART AND DESIGN** Los Angeles, CA "Strategic Difference"
2014	**AIA OMAHA CONFERENCE** Omaha, NE "Building Dichotomies"
2014	**RE-INVENTION CONFERENCE BY ARCHITECT MAGAZINE** Washington D.C. "Post-housing"
2014	**ROME'S MILLENNIUM LECTURE SERIES** Rome, Italy Casa dell' Architettura of the Ordine degli Architetti di Roma "When in Rome"

2013	**MONTANA AIA CONVENTION** Billings, Montana Meeting in the Mountains Conference Keynote Speaker	2008	**UCLA SCHOOL OF ARCHITECTURE** Los Angeles, CA "Beyond Representation"	2012	**COLORADO AIA AWARDS** Denver, CO Jury Chair
2012	**AIA COLORADO STATE CONVENTION** Denver, Colorado "The New Normal" Keynote Speaker	2008	**DWELL ON DESIGN CONFERENCE** Los Angeles, CA "Housing Now"	2012	**INTERNATIONAL GOOD DESIGN AWARDS CHICAGO ATHENAEUM / EUROPEAN CENTRE FOR ARCHITECTURE** Chicago, IL Jury Member
2012	**UNIVERSITY OF MASSACHUSETTS, SCHOOL OF ARCHITECTURE** Amherst, MA "Going Pig"	2007	**SCI-ARC** Los Angeles, CA "In The Rear View Mirror"	2012	**AIA NATIONAL CONVENTION** Washington DC "Excellence in Affordable Housing"
2012	**A+D MUSEUM, CAL POLY METRO PROGRAM** Los Angeles, CA "Seeing is Forgetting"	2007	**AMERICAN ACADEMY IN ROME** Rome, Italy "When In Rome"	2011	**SCI-ARC DISCUSSION WITH ERIC OWEN MOSS** Los Angeles, CA "Out of Memory" panel discussion
		2006	**AIA KANSAS STATE CONVENTION** Topeka, KA "Defining The Current" Keynote Speaker		
2012	**UNIVERSITY OF CINCINNATI, SCHOOL OF ARCHITECTURE** Cincinnati, OH "Differentiated Wholes"	2006	**CAL POLY POMONA** Pomona, CA "Hemostatic Measures"	2010	**DAVID DILLON MEMORIAL** Amherst, Massachusetts Invited Speaker
2012	**PALM SPRINGS MODERNISM WEEK** Palm Springs, CA "A Specific Modernism for the 21st Century"	2006	**CAL STATE LONG BEACH** Long Beach, CA "Objects In Mirror are Larger Than They Appear"	2010	**BIG CITY FORUM #21, GOETHE INSTITUTE** Los Angeles, CA "Shaping LA" Panelist
2012	**COLORADO AIA CONFERENCE** Denver, CO "Recent Inquiries"	2006	**WEST HOLLYWOOD DESIGN NIGHT** West Hollywood, CA "Making Place"	2010	**AIA LOS ANGELES 2X8 STUDENT SCHOLARSHIP AND EXHIBITION** Los Angeles, CA Jury Member
2012	**UNITED STATES INSTITUTE FOR THEATRE TECHNOLOGY CONFERENCE** "White Noise"	2004	**AIA NATIONAL CONVENTION** San Diego, CA "A Grand Small Building, The Collins Gallery"	2010	**MOBIUS AIA LOS ANGELES CONFERENCE ON DESIGN** Los Angeles, CA Roundtable Discussion
2012	**ENVIRONMENTAL CHARTER SCHOOL LOS ANGELES** Los Angeles, CA "Shades of Green"	2002	**UNIVERSITY OF SOUTHERN CALIFORNIA** Los Angeles, CA "Pass Go, Collect 200"	2009	**Pepperdine University Green Leadership Conference** Malibu, CA "Taking it Upstream" Panelist
2011	**STRUCTURES FOR INCLUSION CONFERENCE** Chicago, IL "Re-housing NOW" Keynote Speaker	2001	**LA FORUM FOR ARCHITECTURE OUT THERE DOING IT SERIES** Los Angeles, CA "New Beginning"	2009	**ACSA / ASSOCIATION OF COLLEGIATE SCHOOLS OF ARCHITECTURE CONFERENCE** Portland, OR Paper Peer Reviewer
2009	**AIA ACADEMY OF EMERGING PROFESSIONALS CONFERENCE** Los Angeles, CA "Parts to Whole"		INVITED PANELS AND JURIES	2008	**AIA NEW MEXICO DESIGN AWARDS** Santa Fe, NM Jury Member
		2015	**DENVER AIA AWARDS** Denver, CO Jury Member	2008	**AIA KANSAS DESIGN AWARDS** Topeka, KA Jury Member
2009	**UNIVERSITY OF SOUTHERN CALIFORNIA** Los Angeles, CA "(Re)solution X"	2014	**NEW YORK AIA AWARDS** New York, NY Jury Member	2008	**SCANPH / SOUTHERN CALIFORNIA ASSOCIATION OF NONPROFIT HOUSING CONFERENCE** Los Angeles, CA "New Housing Typologies" Panelist
2009	**WOODBURY UNIVERSITY** Glendale, CA "In Between/Place"	2014	**AIA LOS ANGELES 2X8 STUDENT SCHOLARSHIP AND EXHIBITION** Los Angeles, CA Jury Member		
2009	**MOCA CONTEMPORARIES** Los Angeles, CA Tour and Discussion / Moving Picture Company	2013	**UNIVERSITY OF SOUTHERN CALIFORNIA** Los Angeles, CA "The Future of Housing in Los Angeles" Panelist	2007	**MOBIUS CONFERENCE ON DESIGN LOS ANGELES** Los Angeles, CA "Affordable Housing" Panelist
				2007	**MOBIUS CONFERENCE ON DESIGN LOS ANGELES** Los Angeles, CA "Sustainable Solutions" Panelist
2008	**AIA ARIZONA CONFERENCE** Phoenix, AZ "Problem (RE)solved" Keynote Speaker	2012	**CHICAGO ARCHITECTURE FOUNDATION** Chicago, IL "Design for Social Change" Panelist	2006	**AIA NATIONAL CONVENTION** Los Angeles, CA "Young Architects Roundtable" Panelist